CAJUN COUNTRY
CHRONICLES

CAJUN COUNTRY
CHRONICLES

William J. Thibodeaux

THE
History
PRESS

Published by The History Press
Charleston, SC
www.historypress.com

Front cover, top left: Ms. Comeaux's students at Atchafalaya school, circa 1938. High water was a frequent visitor. *Courtesy of René Prejean. Top, center*: Varise Conner, "the greatest unrecorded Cajun musician," standing in front of his sawmill in Lake Arthur. *Courtesy of Mitch Conner, youngest of Varise's seven children. Top, right*: Atchafalaya was a maze of elevated walkways where mud and splinters were a common part of life. Tom Bernard owned several businesses in the basin. *Courtesy of René Prejean. Bottom*: Thrashing rice in Cajun country near Crowley, Louisiana. *Courtesy of Freeland Archives and Acadia Parish library in Crowley, Louisiana. Back cover*: Setting sun in swamp scene at Lake Martin. *Courtesy of Susie Trahan of Lafayette, formerly of Gueydan, Louisiana.*

First published 2023

Manufactured in the United States

ISBN 9781467155298

Library of Congress Control Number: 2023938578

Notice: The information in this book is true and complete to the best of our knowledge. It is offered without guarantee on the part of the author or The History Press. The author and The History Press disclaim all liability in connection with the use of this book.

CONTENTS

ACKNOWLEDGEMENTS

I am eternally grateful to my wife, Judy, for her invaluable support and encouragement in all my endeavors. She has been especially understanding and patient with me while I spend countless hours researching, interviewing and writing and rewriting material, both for this book and other work. This book is especially dedicated to Ms. Patricia Segura of Abbeville, who often encouraged me to write a book. During the autumn of her life, she edited many of my articles before sending them to the publisher. She is dearly missed by her friends and family. This book is also dedicated to an old friend and videographer extraordinaire, Jack Winn of Lafayette. For years, Jack unselfishly volunteered his time and video recorded many of my interviews, lectures and book talks, especially in the earlier years. Due to other commitments and family obligations, he was compelled to give it up.

I am also grateful to the following: Arcadia Publishing and The History Press, especially my commissioning editor, Joe Gartrell, and my copyeditor, Zoe Ames.

Newspaper archives for preserving our Louisiana history

Susie and Michael Shanahan of Sapulpa, Oklahoma

Gene Thibodeaux of Church Point

Ms. Ann Mire of Crowley

Acadia Parish Library staff of Crowley and the tireless genealogy workers

Freeman Archives

Dorothy B. McNeely of Crowley

Genealogy Trails History Group
Larry G. Miller of Iowa
Curtis Joubert of Eunice
John Leleux of Crowley
Louis J. Perret, Lafayette Parish clerk of court, and the wonderful
    courthouse staff
John "Pudd" Sharp of Lafayette
Norma and Franklin Price of Lake Arthur
Harriet Shultz of Jennings and her wonderful staff at Carnegie Library
Louis K. Broussard of Milton
Jerry Clark of Morse
Alvin Bethard of Lafayette
Robert "Bob" Broussard of Centerville
Joseph "J.C." Moreaux of Houston
William "Bill" Lamar of Morgan City
Ray "Dup" Duplechain of Belle Chasse
Heidi Carline of Gueydan
Celena Breaux of Gueydan
Helen Gaspard Hayes of Gueydan
Rosa Lepretre of Riceville
Eric Castille of Lafayette
Bevan Brothers Photography of Eunice
Deen Thomas
Herman Venable of Lafayette
Vermilion Parish Library staff of Abbeville
Ann and Eddie Palmer of Lafayette
Pat Daigle of Church Point
Paul and Mona Daigle of Church Point
Robert and Vicki and Josh Elkins of Church Point
Ann and Mark Savoy of Eunice
Elton "Bee" Cormier
Terry Badin of Gueydan
Elwood Cormier of Lafayette
Jane Matte of Lafayette
Warren Perrin of Erath
Francis Comeaux of Lafayette
Barry Ancelet of Scott
Gail Langley Dufrene of Des Allemands
Dr. Rick Fremaux of St. Martinville

The late Pierre Varmon Daigle of Church Point
Brenda Daigle of Youngsville
Gercie Daigle of Church Point
Kelly Hebert of Church Point
James Akers of St. Martinville
Richard Landry of Lafayette
Melvin Robin of Maurice
Mitch Conner of Lake Arthur
Pattie Dupuis of Abbeville
Terry Dupuis of St. Martinville
The wonderful St. Martinville parish library staff
Marianne and Adam Conque of St. Martinville
Richard DesHotels of Baton Rouge
Mason John "Boss" Voss

INTRODUCTION

Cajun Country Chronicles is a collection of fascinating nonfictional vignettes that chronicles Louisiana's enormous and diverse history and heritage. These pages are chock-full of interesting and historical information from a bygone era of actual events with real people of Louisiana. Some date to the antebellum period, but most take place during the 1800s and early 1900s. They are twice-told stories, since they were buried in newsprint and forgotten. They have since been disinterred and are now being retold in a practical writing style using everyday language.

Chapter 1

THE ST. MARTINVILLE CURSE

In March 1893, a curse was reportedly placed on the town of St. Martinville by a condemned man who protested his innocence until the end. The condemned man allegedly said, "Until justice is done, the town will not prosper; grass will grow in the streets, and nothing will thrive." St. Martinville—or Le Petit Paris, as it was sometimes referred to back then—is one of Louisiana's oldest communities. It was originally named the Poste des Attakapas. It was settled in the eighteenth century and incorporated in 1815. The vast area of Attakapas consisted of 5,100 square miles and formed an irregular triangle, which encompassed an area from the Atchafalaya River to the Mermentau River and the Gulf of Mexico. Attakapas was later divided into the parishes of St. Martin, St. Mary, Lafayette, Vermilion, Iberia and part of Cameron.

The railroad came to St. Martinville about mid-1882, one year before the completion of the second transcontinental railroad that traversed Acadiana and two years before its arrival in Vermilionville (Lafayette). Along with the railroad came a horde of railroad men. Many of them brought their families, which was the case for Southern Pacific Railroad civil engineer James S. Robertson. He and his wife, Mary, and Isabelle, James Robertson's adult daughter from a previous marriage, accompanied Mr. and Mrs. Robertson to St. Martinville from Centralia, Illinois. According to St. Martinville historian James Akers, the Robertson family purchased an 1830 Greek Revival home on the banks of the leisurely flowing Bayou Teche. The large, white two-story home with its white picket fence was conveniently located

Left: James Akers (*second from right, with white shirt and ballcap*) holding court outside of the Acadian Memorial and Museum in St. Martinville. James is the preeminent historian of St. Martinville. *Author's collection.*

Opposite: The Evangeline Oak. *Author's collection.*

near the railroad depot. The home was built by Paul Briant, a Frenchman from Santo Domingo, now named Haiti. Briant later became the first judge in St. Martin Parish.

James Robertson was killed in a railroad accident. Accidents on the railroad during that era were quite frequent and often deadly. Most railroad jobs were dangerous, especially during the link and pin era. Back then, when someone wanted a job on the railroad, the hiring railroad official would often say, "Show me your hands." If the prospective railroader/ employee didn't have a finger or two maimed or missing, he didn't have experienced hands and subsequently wasn't hired. For income, Mrs. James Robertson and her adult stepdaughter Isabelle, also known as Miss Belle, took in boarders. Travelers called their place the Evangeline Hotel, while railroaders called it home.

Sometime during the night of Tuesday, August 11, 1891, both women were brutally and savagely murdered. On August 15, 1891, the local newspaper in St. Martinville reported that at about seven o'clock in the morning on August 12, 1891, neighbors noticed the Robertson home was still shut, which was unusual. The two trainmen who rented rooms there didn't see the two women in the home, and their bedroom doors were closed. They knocked, but there was no answer from within. Policeman C.H. Voorhies was notified, entered the home, opened the door to the bedroom and found the gruesome murder scene. On August 18, 1891, a New Orleans newspaper reported that a week after the double murders, Louis Michel, who had "a very unsavory reputation," was arrested in Plaquemine, Louisiana, the previous day (August 17). Five days later (Saturday, August 22, 1891), Deputy Sheriff A.V. Fleming arrived in St.

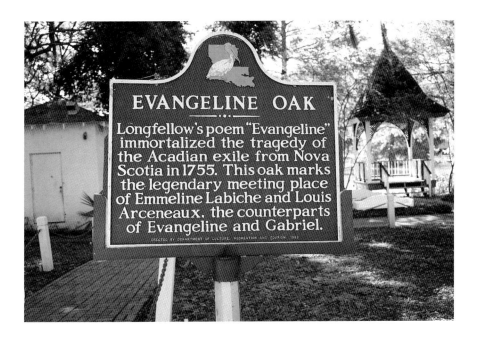

Martinville from Plaquemine with Louis Michel as his prisoner. Michel was locked behind bars with Lewis Chambers, who was arrested some time earlier.

On September 24, 1882, the local newspaper of St. Martinville reported that the trial got underway on the previous Monday, September 19. Although the trial had all the elements of intrigue and mystery, it was a false start. One of the witnesses from New Orleans for the defense wasn't present, and defense attorney Edward Simon objected. A bench warrant was issued, a deputy sheriff was sent to retrieve the witness and on Tuesday evening, the deputy arrived with his man. So, it's fair to say the court case against the two began on Wednesday, September 21, 1892. At the time, defense attorney Simon was a prominent lawyer in St. Martinville. When he was a student at Harvard University, he studied under Simon Greenleaf (1783–1853), one of the founding fathers of Harvard Law School and one of the greatest legal scholars of his time. He also studied with Judge Joseph Story (1779–1845), who served on the U.S. Supreme Court. Young Simon also studied American literature with poet Henry Wadsworth Longfellow (1807–1882). Simon was never credited as the source of information for Longfellow's epic poem *Evangeline*, although Longfellow did credit his friend Nathaniel Hawthorne (1804–1864) as the source for his legendary masterpiece. It's doubtful that Longfellow or Hawthorne ever set foot

Attorney/judge Edward Simon informed Wadsworth Longfellow about the plight of the Acadian exiles, and Simon was never credited. *Author's collection.*

St. Martin Parish's courthouse was originally built in 1853, and over the years, there were ten additions to the original structure. It was last added onto in 2010. *Author's collection.*

anywhere near St. Martinville, Louisiana. Longfellow got his information from Émile Edouard (Edward) Simon II (1824–1914), the defense attorney representing Michel and Chambers. I digressed a bit to inform readers about Judge Edward Simon's early years. Now, back to the jury trial of Louis Michel and Lewis Chambers.

On Wednesday, September 21, 1892, the entire day was taken up by selecting a jury, which was completed by five o'clock in the afternoon. The court session convened Thursday morning at nine o'clock, "at which time the taking of evidence commenced" while the accused sat and listened attentively. The entire jury was made up of fair-skinned men, most sporting large muttonchop sideburns and fin de siècle mustaches under their stiff-crowned hats as others fingered their shaggy full beards, probably smoking Daniel Webster cigars. During that period, women and Blacks did not serve on juries. Members of the jury were W.H. Livingston, Willie Potier, Paul Halphen, Arthur Patin, Placide Huval, Ambroise Deguretaire, Alfred Delonne, Rosembert Dupuis, Sidney Lastrapes, Jules Hebert, Chas Rees Jr. and Fred Schmidt. The trial closed Saturday evening, and the jurors retired to their room for deliberation and remained there until Monday. When Monday came, the jury rendered an "unqualified verdict" of guilty, which is the legal definition of guilty by verdict. It also meant death by hanging for the two men. No courtroom details of the trial were mentioned in any newspaper articles.

I was reminded of the adage "be careful what you wish for" when I learned that Chambers asked his attorney to file a motion for a new trial. It was granted by the trial judge Jas E. Mouton, with the consent of District Attorney T.D. Foster. Not to be outdone, Louis Michel appealed to the Louisiana supreme court for a new trial, and the tribunal reversed the lower court's decision and granted one to Michel. No reason was given for the granting of a new trial, other than the possibility of the prosecution winning a sentence of death at the second try. It was an audacious challenge. Some felt it was a dubious exercise. It was risky, a gamble, a roll of the dice and perhaps even snake eyes. Gaining a new trial somewhat lifted the spirits of Michel and Chambers.

The second trial for two of the three men accused of murdering the two Robertson women got underway. The jury was again composed of all-White men. They were Auguste Barras, Casimir Wiltz, John Coles, D. Champagne, Victor Maraist, Adolph Orillion, Emile Martin, L. Louis Legrand, P. Barras, John Franz, Alfred Geoffroy and P. Dwyer. The jury proceedings for Louis Michel and Lewis Chambers indicated the jurors went into their chamber to deliberate at 7:25 on Saturday evening. A decision wasn't reached, so it was decided to resume at 9:00 a.m. Monday morning. The headline of the weekly newspaper of October 1, 1892, read, "The jury stood ten for a verdict of guilty and two for guilty without capital punishment." The two holdouts held on until they decided "to render an unqualified verdict of guilty!" Unqualified verdict! The accused didn't comprehend the curious legal jargon. A guilty verdict with the word *qualified* meant without capital punishment, while an unqualified verdict indicated that both men would go to the gallows.

Chambers and Michel's attorneys again requested an appeal of the state supreme court, but the high court sided with the lower court's decision and declined. According to the local paper of December 10, 1892, the decision by the Louisiana supreme court was delivered by Associate Justice McEnery, the same McEnery appointed governor of Louisiana after the death of Governor Wiltz in 1881. He was later elected Louisiana governor in 1884. The recent decision weighed heavily on the two convicted men. It was an unusually cold winter in south Louisiana, according to the local weekly newspaper of December 31, 1892, which reported "the first cold this winter....The mercury fell as low as 20 degrees below freezing point." In the same publication was an appeal by defense attorney Edward Simon asking for yet another trial for Louis Michel and Lewis Chambers. The two were previously sentenced to death and their sentences confirmed by the state supreme court. The evidence used against the two men was circumstantial. This was the first death sentence rendered since the War Between the States. The newspaper reported that Michel was undisturbed when hearing the verdict. He was aloof, while Chambers, on the other hand, was badly disturbed. He used harsh language against a doctor who was present at the time when informed of the verdict. He had a wistful expression, with sorrowful eyes.

The local newspaper of St. Martinville dated January 21, 1893, reported that the daughters of Lewis Chambers were circulating a petition "to have the sentence of their father commuted to the penitentiary for life" instead of hanging. The publication continued by stating there was some doubt in the community as to the guilt of Chambers, "or at least in the evidence against Chambers." However, he had been convicted twice; they were battling a seemingly insurmountable and elusive endeavor. The newspaper doubted any of the jurors would sign the petition. Regarding the first trial, "The jury stood eleven for capital punishment and one for a qualified verdict"—without capital punishment.

Left: St. Martinville Acadian Memorial and Museum. *Author's collection.*

Below: Acadian Memorial Mural, the arrival of Acadians depicted by Robert Dafford. *Author's collection.*

The local newspaper of March 4, 1983, reported that representatives of the *Messenger* and the *New Delta*, accompanied by Sheriff Rees and other citizens, interviewed the condemned men. The two men were willing to talk. The reporter for the *Messenger* blurted out they would be executed on Friday, March 24, 1893. It was almost as if the correspondent took great enjoyment in informing the two condemned men. The men said they never expected justice, "but God knows that we are innocent."

The *Clarion* of Opelousas dated March 11, 1893, informed its readers that on March 1, 1893, Governor Foster (the first one) signed the death warrants for the executions to be carried out on Friday, March 24, 1893, between the hours of eleven and four o'clock. The *Messenger* reported that Judge Jas. K. Mouton presided at the first trial and Mr. T.D. Foster, district attorney, represented the state. During the second trial, Judge Felix Voorhies presided, and District Attorney R.F. Broussard represented the state. The newspaper reported that all the evidence produced at both trials against the two prisoners was "wholly and entirely circumstantial, there was not a single direct piece of evidence brought against either of the accused." On August 11, 1891, the night of the double murders, it was said that Lewis Chambers and a couple of other Black men were hired to listen from under the house to determine which political candidates the Robertson women were supporting—although it was never determined who the candidates were or what they were running for. But at about the time the get-together ended, the men were seen coming out from under the house, and the townsfolk remembered the incident, put two and two together and convicted Lewis Chambers and Louis Michel. This was the only bit of evidence used. Times were much different during the late 1800s than they are today. Back then a man, especially a Black man, could be convicted of nearly anything. The paper also reported that "several other negroes and colored women were arrested and jailed but were subsequently released." Meanwhile, the search for Paul Cormier, the third Black man believed to be part of the gang that viciously killed the Robertson women, continued.

The *Messenger* of March 11, 1893, reported that visitors to Louis Michel's jail cell would often find him on his knees praying with an open Bible. Chambers was visited by his wife on Monday, "the first time since the days of February." T.J. Labbe, a reporter with the *Delta*, visited both prisoners along with jailer Eugene Bertrand. Both prisoners were happy to have visitors. It eased the boredom of imprisonment. Since their conviction, they had plenty of visitors on most days. Although the men understood the severity of their predicament, they both claimed their innocence. One of Chambers's

Setting sun over Lake Martin. *Photo courtesy of Susie Trahan of Lafayette, formerly of Gueydan.*

sisters visited her brother and said the petition to save his life was proceeding well. Louis Michel claimed this wasn't about him killing anyone. "It was about an old grudge the people had against him which dated back 22 years." The *Messenger* of March 11, 1883, reported that it was about 1873, shortly after the Reconstruction period in Louisiana, when Louis Michel held a high position in the Republican Party. During that period after the loss of the war, scalawags and carpetbaggers flooded the state of Louisiana. Subsequently, Alcibiades DeBlanc (1821–1883), a former Confederate lieutenant colonel of the Eighth Infantry, created the Knights of the White Camellia, which was like the Knights of the Ku Klux Klan. This was before the 1876 election of Rutherford B. Hayes and "one of the most acrimonious presidential elections in American history" argued Hampton Sides, a noted American historian and best-selling author of several great books, including *In the Kingdom of Ice*. Sides continued, "Many Democrats refused to consider his [Hayes's] presidency legitimate, calling him 'Rutherfraud.'" The above resulted in the Compromise of 1877, and as a concession to Louisiana, Francis T. Nichols, a former brigadier general of the Confederacy, was named governor of Louisiana. Nichols won the election outright, but the Republican Party refused to seat him. After Hayes's controversial presidential election, to smooth things out, he recognized the Democrat Nicholls as the winner. Regardless of the compromise, Nicholls won the election fair and square by eight thousand votes.

The weekly local newspaper of St. Martinville dated March 18, 1893, reported that the two condemned men were prepared to die in just several more days. Their families were now visiting them daily. The two men had a haircut and shave a week earlier and asked for another shave on the day of their execution. Louis Michel was often found in his cell kneeling in front of a chair that held an open Bible, holding beads in his hand, fervently praying. He told a reporter that a few nights earlier, he was awakened by voices that sang sweetly; he saw Jesus Christ and the Virgin Mary surrounded by angels who opened the doors of heaven. Louis Michel said Jesus Christ was his witness that he was innocent and knew nothing of the murders. "The Noose!" On March 25, 1893, the *Weekly Messenger* (St. Martinville, Louisiana) recapped the murder scene of two years earlier, beginning by stating it was known that the two women had company in the house until about ten o'clock the night of the murders. According to James Akers of St. Martinville, on the night of the murders, the Robertson women were having a political get-together. After all, this was during the Progressive Era, a time of social activism and political reform across the country. Back then, as it is today in Louisiana, politics was a favorite sport—like football and baseball!

After the murder of the two Robertson women, the disappearance of the third Black man, Paul Cormier, raised suspicions; he was seen the night of the murders but absconded and disappeared without any clues to his whereabouts. He was believed to be in a number of places with one of the assassins and in the company of Louis Michel, alias Louis Broussard. It was also learned that Louis Michel was seen in St. Martinville despite

Swamp scene in Lake Martin: a great egret preparing for supper. *Photo courtesy of Susie Trahan of Lafayette, formerly of Gueydan.*

having been banned from entering St. Martin Parish by the Regulators. The Regulators was a vigilante group that made sure everyone obeyed the law—and, in most cases, was the law. The vigilantes came into power during Reconstruction, after the War Between the States. It was a time when Louisiana was littered with carpetbaggers and the law was nearly nonexistent. The same newspaper article reported that the day of the murder, Louis Michel was seen at Fause Pointe and Jeanerette with a bag of money the Cajuns referred to as *argent blanc* (coins), which he tried to exchange for bills. An unidentified person matching the description of Paul Cormier accompanied Michel. The sheriff of St. Martin Parish was notified that Louis Michel was in Plaquemine, Louisiana. He quickly sent a telegraph message to Sheriff Brusle of Iberville Parish to arrest Michel and to hold him until a deputy from St. Martinville could come for him. The arresting officer in Plaquemine said Michel was in the company of another Black man who matched the description of Paul Cormier, but there was no warrant out for his arrest.

The investigators at the Robertson home said robbery was the likely motive. Mrs. Jas S. Robertson's throat was slashed from ear to ear, while Isabelle J. Robertson was strangled to death. The ladies had adjoining rooms upstairs, and both of the women were found dead in Mrs. Robertson's room. Investigators surmised that the older woman was murdered first and perhaps made noise, which caused Isabelle to enter the room, and that was when the younger woman was strangled. The bedding was soaked in blood. The elder Mrs. Robertson's jugular vein had been severed as she lay on her bed. The body of Isabella was found on the floor next to her stepmother's bed. An impression of the fingerprints of one of the murderers was found on Isabella's neck. The two women put up a struggle to save their lives. Mrs. Robertson was about seventy years of age, and Isabelle was forty years old.

At the time of the murders, two boarders, Phillip Coyne and Chas Doer, were in their rooms sleeping and didn't report hearing anything unusual. The two men worked as locomotive engineer and brakeman, respectively, on Southern Pacific's newly built branch line, the St. Martinville Branch. Coyne's room was on the second floor opposite Isabelle's room and separated from it by a six-foot corridor, while Doer's room was downstairs. Being a locomotive engineer and a brakeman, operating noisy locomotives and shrieking train whistles, both men probably suffered from hearing loss. It's been an occupational hazard for most U.S. railroaders, especially trainmen and enginemen.

Swamp scene at beautiful Lake Martin. *Photo courtesy of Jack Winn of Lafayette.*

On Friday, March 24, 1893, only one man would hang for the murders, and that would be Louis Michel. Meanwhile, Lewis Chambers was granted a reprieve while waiting on a decision of the Louisiana parole board "for a communication of his sentence." So, his sisters' petition paid off! Louis Michel reportedly had a good night's sleep and a hearty breakfast. He was given communion by a priest, and at eleven thirty, he was taken to the gallows. The priest followed behind. Sheriff Rees read the death warrant. After the warrant was read, the sheriff asked Michel if he wanted to talk. Michel asked the sheriff to remove his cigar so he could speak, since his arms were tied. A crowd of somewhere between "six hundred and a thousand people" was in attendance. However, only fifteen witnesses were allowed in the enclosure to witness the execution. They were Gabriel Grevemberg, James E. Mouton, Theophile Elmer, Laurent Ducrest, Anatole Cormier, Dr. A.C. Durio, Clairville Bienvenu, Taylor Daspit, Jos. Rees, Emanual Liviachi, C.M. Olivier, Adolphe Cormier, Arcade Ganthier, Paulin Guidry and Sheriff Rees and his deputies, along with newspaper reporters. Michel looked hale and hearty, a formidable figure. When allowed to speak to the crowd, he first spoke in English and then in French. He had a drink of water and wine and said a prayer. He also asked the people to please not take it out on his wife, as this was about him, and to please help see that she had food to survive.

The last prayer was said at 12:17, his legs were fettered at 12:19, the noose was placed around Louis Michel's neck and "the black cap was placed over his head at 12:20 p.m." The trapdoor was sprung, and Michel entered the underworld of eternity. The fall was said to be about six feet, and his neck was broken. It was ominously silent; all that was heard was the tick and groan of the taut rope as the sound resonated. The newspaper reported there were only "two slight twitches" of Michel's body. "At 12:35 he was pronounced dead and at 1:05 the body was cut down and placed in a plain cypress coffin. He was buried the same evening at 3 o'clock." Louis Michel was tall, a little stoop-shouldered and forty-two years of age. He left behind his wife, Celestine E. Michel, "and several children, some were adults."

The *Weekly Messenger*, on April 1, 1893, reported that Albert Bienvenu, editor and proprietor of St. Martinville's weekly publication, was pleased to report he had an extra-large edition especially for this day, the day of Louis Michel's execution. Bienvenu said it was a very successful day for his publication. On April 15, 1893, in an article headlined "An Important Capture," the *Weekly Messenger* reported that a newspaper boy in Houston spotted Paul Cormier at the Southern Pacific train depot. Cormier was alleged to be the third man who helped kill the Robertson women two years earlier. The alleged killer was finally captured by Houston police and jailed. The newspaper also reported that the newsboy was placed in the cell with Cormier to try to obtain more information from him, but he was not talking. At the bottom of the publication was a disclaimer from the *Lafayette Advertiser* that argued, "The publication of the above article created quite a sensation here. Sheriff Rees telegraphed Houston for information, and the reply says there is no foundation for the article. It is a 'canard.'"

During an economic depression referred to as the Panic of 1893, which affected every sector of the United States, a newspaper headline read, "Lewis Chambers Commuted." The *Weekly Messenger* of June 3, 1893, reported that Chambers's sentence was commuted by the governor of Louisiana. There was "too much doubt" about his involvement with the Robertson murder case "for a death penalty." Chambers's sentence was commuted to life in prison at hard labor. His sisters' persistence with the petition had indeed paid off. People in St. Martinville were surprised when they noticed Lewis Chambers pass through town with Sheriff Rees on his way to the railroad station to take the train to the penitentiary at Baton Rouge. In the same publication, there was an announcement by the *Morning Star and Catholic Messenger* that read, in part, "Circumstantial evidence must convince beyond reasonable doubt before the jury ought to convict." The article continued,

"Other mistakes may be rectified and made good. The mistakes that result in death is final and irreparable. It is better that ninety and nine guilty escape than that one innocent man should perish."

Numerous people believed that Louis Michel was hanged twice. According to my old friend James Akers from St. Martinville, he had it on good authority that when Michel dropped through the opening in the floor of the gallows, the rope was too long, and Michel was reported to be extremely tall. When Michel's feet landed on solid earth, he was alleged to be still very much alive. James Akers said, "An alert jailer by the name of Eugene Bertrand grabbed a nearby shovel and started digging beneath the feet of Louis Michel where he died a slow and agonizing death." As I've stated earlier, the evidence used against Louis Michel and Lewis Chambers was entirely circumstantial; not one sliver of hard evidence was produced to convict the men. Nowhere in the pile of newsprint was there a disparaging word, a hint of malice or vulgarity or a curse on the town of St. Martinville from Louis Michel, who supposedly placed a curse on the town before he was hanged. It was purely the product of someone's wild and vivid imagination.

This majestic home was the scene of a double murder in the late 1800s. It was originally built by Paul Briant, who later became the first judge of St. Martinville. Later it was owned by Dr. Willie Bienvenu. The current owners are Marianne and Adam Conque. *Author's collection.*

James Akers said the Robertson family home was later sold to Mrs. Luke Bonin, grandmother of Dr. Willie Bienvenu. Willie lived in the mansion and worked directly across the street at the hospital. The house later became known as the Bienvenu House. This was during the time that Southern Pacific Railroad announced it was about to begin construction on the Royville (Youngsville) branch from Cade to Royville. Sometime later, the old plantation home was sold and renamed the Bienvenue House Bed and Breakfast. The story doesn't end here. Slightly more than four years after the horrific murder of the Robertson women, someone had information to share with Sheriff Rees. Under the title "Local News," the *Weekly Messenger* of August 25, 1894, reported that Sheriff Rees returned from St. Landry Parish after meeting with an informant who knew the name of the third man believed to have committed the murders with Louis Michel and Lewis Chambers. Although, he described Paul Cormier in precise detail, the informant said this man called himself Paul Jones. This "Paul Jones" informed him about a murder he was involved in with others. He described how much trouble he and his coconspirators had "coming down through the window on a ladder." The informant also said he had met this Paul Jones, a.k.a. Paul Cormier, earlier in the year in Algiers, where he was living with his wife. Somehow, nothing panned out with this Paul Jones, and the investigation went dormant again.

Fast-forward twenty years. The *Weekly Messenger* of June 3, 1911, reported St. Martin Parish sheriff E.A. Broussard and Deputy F. Champagne arrested Paul Cormier, aka Paul Bras Courts, in Oklahoma, where he was well ensconced. It was the Gordian knot of identities. The same newspaper, a week later, reported that despite this man having all the features of Cormier—e.g., short arms, skin color, scars and marks on his head, body and arms—no one could positively identify him as Cormier. It was reported that all the evidence in the case was about the same as in the trial of Louis Michel and Lewis Chambers but with a different outcome. Paul Cormier or Paul Bras Courts (whichever was his name) was acquitted of all charges. The jury felt there was some doubt as to Cormier's positive identification. At about that same time, it was reported that several years earlier, Lewis Chambers was released from prison after serving out his time for his part in the alleged murders of the Robertson women. Slightly more than four months later, the *New Iberia Enterprise and Independent* newspaper reported that despite the fugitive (Cormier) being on the run for twenty years, the sheriff's witnesses positively identified Cormier by his general features. The trial for Paul Cormier alias Paul Bras Courts got underway, and once again, the jury

The preeminent historian James Akers of St. Martinville (*right*). *Author's collection.*

consisted of all White males. They were Dumas Bernard, Carlos Bienvenu, Geo. Livingston, Drauzin Augelle, A.G. Broussard, Vincent Barras, Jos. Angelle, A. Potier, S. Cormier, Frank Babin, F. Kershehenter and A. Guidry. There were more than one hundred witnesses at the trial, and the court worked late into the night.

The old rail line that once traversed through St. Martinville no longer exists. It was where this author cut his teeth on railroad track inspection in the 1970s. The rails were removed sometime in the 1980s, along with other railroad branch lines. My old friend James Akers informed me that five years before the Robertson murders, Cormier had killed a merchant named Simon in Thibodaux. I searched but could not find any information regarding this incident. Akers also informed me that years later in Morgan City, long after the trials, one of the two railroad men who was at the Robertson home at the time of the murders made a deathbed confession stating he had murdered the two women.

Chapter 2

A SHORT HISTORY
OF LOUISIANA

In 1803, within a twenty-day span—twenty days!—the Louisiana Territory went from Spanish rule to French rule and, finally, to American rule. The land sale included about 827,000 square miles for $15 million, which equates to about $18 per square mile. To get a better perspective of the enormity of this land mass, it included all or parts of fourteen states in today's middle America, including Louisiana, Texas, Oklahoma, Arkansas, Missouri, Iowa, Minnesota, Kansas, South Dakota, North Dakota, Montana, Wyoming, Colorado and New Mexico. It doubled the size of the United States and was said to be Thomas Jefferson's crowning achievement during his presidency. Two hundred years after the fact, people are still asking if the Louisiana Purchase was legal. That is an age-old question that has been asked innumerable times.

The present state of Louisiana is between the thirty-third-degree parallel of north latitude to the Gulf of Mexico and from the Sabine River to the Pearl River. It is composed of 48,506 square miles with the average elevation at one hundred feet, but a great deal of the land mass is much lower. The highest point is in the northwestern part of the state, reaching upward of 500 feet. The majority of information for this chapter of the book is from Garnie William McGinty (1900–1984). He was a native Louisianian and taught history for thirty years. For twenty of those years, McGinty was slowly compiling information for his excellent work *A History of Louisiana*, published in 1949. He taught history at what was then called Louisiana Polytechnic Institute at Ruston, Louisiana. Today, the school is named Louisiana Tech

Sun setting over
Lake Martin. *Photo
courtesy of Susie
Trahan of Lafayette,
formerly of Gueydan.*

University. In his book, McGinty wrote that Louisiana has "more miles of navigable streams than any other state."

Contrary to what we've been told, the British weren't the first explorers to reach North America. McGinty said the college in Mexico City named the Royal and Pontifical University of Mexico "was six decades old when John Smith and his companions were starving on the banks of the James River." He argued that Spanish explorers were building colonies before the British settled at Jamestown. McGinty claimed that our laws of today are based on the laws of Paris; even legal procedure and community property was inherited from the French government. Louisiana, having obtained its inheritance laws from the Romans, is the only state where children of the deceased are required to be included as heirs. Even in court proceedings back then, "litigants did not have to hire a lawyer, make bond, or pay court fees."

In Louisiana and probably elsewhere, slaves could not own property, and they could not give testimony in court either for or against their masters. A slave could not bring a complaint to court. However, he could give testimony in court, but only in the absence of a White witness. On the other hand, a slave could not be prosecuted without the slave owner "being made a party." Any slave that "struck his master, mistress, or their children" was subject to be put to death. A slave owner was held liable for the dishonesty of his slave, and if he failed to pay whatever damages there might be, he forfeited ownership. Married slaves were not to be sold separately. And if a plantation was sold or seized, the slaves stayed with the land. Children of slaves below the age of fourteen were not to be separated from their mothers.

The meandering Bayou Teche. *Author's collection.*

The French quarter of New Orleans is bounded by the Mississippi River and Esplanade, Rampart and Canal Streets. However, years ago, when New Orleans was being developed, it originally consisted of sixty-six square blocks—hence the name Vieux Carré, or "old square." At that time, there were perhaps fewer than five thousand White inhabitants in Louisiana.

Biloxi was the capital, but it was inconvenient, so the capital was moved to New Orleans in 1722. Some decades later, and while the state was under French rule, Jews were forbidden in Louisiana. This was also the case in many areas of the country.

I'll digress a bit to mention that it is a known fact that New Englanders helped the British drive off the Acadians from old Acadie in 1755. Some years earlier, the terms of the Treaty of Ryswick in 1697, when peace was restored, called for "mutual restoration of all conquests," which meant Acadie was restored to the French. New Englanders were bitterly opposed to this part of the treaty. They probably didn't need much persuasion in assisting the British during the Acadians' expulsion in 1755. And just to be clear, the deportation had nothing to do with a pledge of loyalty to the British Crown—it was all about the land. While on the subject of Acadie, in 1703, Iberville persuaded the French government to send a shipload of women to Acadie. Before this, Acadie was inhabited by men and Native Americans. Some of the Frenchmen were known as *coureurs de bois* (runners of the woods.) In 1726, Bienville did for New Orleans what Iberville had done earlier in old Acadie. He requested and arranged with the Ursuline Sisters to send "French peasant girls of good character and robust health" to Louisiana. And so, in 1728 the women were provided with small boxes for their belongings. The parcels apparently looked like small coffins, so the women were referred to as *filles à la cassette* or casket girls. Bienville, the Father of Louisiana, left and returned to France. During that period, it took anywhere from one to three months to cross the Atlantic from New Orleans to France or vice versa.

The first sugarcane was planted in Louisiana in 1700, some "eighteen leagues [about fifty-four miles] from the mouth of the Mississippi River." However, perhaps the land was unfavorable, because sugarcane didn't grow—at least, according to McGinty, not until "the Jesuits introduced it in 1751." This was about the time that the French government gave Louisiana land grants, which were allotted by Bienville's replacement, Canadian-born Governor de Vaudreuil. Vaudreuil gave would-be farmers "eight to ten arpents fronting the Mississippi River," which extended out toward the swamp forty to fifty arpents. An arpent is a French unit of measurement and is approximately 0.84 acres. The land was far from being free, not monetarily but work-wise. A prospective farmer had to build a levee along the river to protect against overflow. He had to maintain a good road parallel to the levee, and he had to dig a drainage ditch beside the road. Three years later, in 1753, Vaudreuil returned to Canada, where he was appointed governor.

On November 3, 1762, a secret deal (the Treaty of Fontainebleau) was completed between France and Spain, whereby Spain now ruled "the territory of Louisiana west of the Mississippi, and the Isle of Orleans." The reason for the exchange was said to be that it was too costly to maintain Louisiana. Strange as it may seem, the territory of Louisiana belonged to the Spanish but remained French. The Acadians were surprised when they learned of this when they arrived in Louisiana about 1764, thinking it was still ruled by the French. The Acadians continued to arrive in Louisiana until about 1785.

The Spanish government gave land grants much like the French. However, the amount of land was forty arpents, and the grantee had to promise to build and maintain a levee, construct a road and fencing and clear the land within a specified time. Toward the end of their occupation, the Spanish gave larger grants, which caused a controversy at the time of the Louisiana Purchase. The disagreement was finally settled with a treaty with Spain in 1819. All land grants up to 1818 were honored. Most inhabitants were agrarian settlers. They worked the soil and tended to their animals. By 1800, New Orleans was "the gateway for most of the trade," and Catholicism was the dominant religion, with a sprinkling of Protestants.

In 1794, two Spaniards, Mendez and Solis, devised a new way to market their sugarcane. One turned the sugarcane juice into syrup, while the other turned his into rum. A year later, Étienne de Boré turned his sugarcane into sugar. Other planters followed Étienne. New Orleans suffered two great fires,

Great egret in the swamps of Lake Martin preparing to catch its supper. *Photo courtesy of Susie Trahan of Lafayette, formerly of Gueydan.*

one in 1788, which was the worst. More than two hundred buildings were destroyed, along with every store but two. Food shortages were extreme. The other fire was in 1794. According to McGinty, the last Spanish governor of Louisiana was Juan Manuel de Salcedo. In 1802, an undisclosed turn of events (the Treaty of San Ildefonso) between Napoleon and Spain took place, and Louisiana was returned to France. However, Juan Manuel de Salcedo, the Spanish governor, continued to rule until November 30, 1903. That was seven months after Napoleon sold Louisiana to the United States and "only 20 days before the actual transfer." It is as confusing now as it must have been back then. Things were happening fast behind the scenes that involved Napoleon, England and a slave revolt in Haiti. The latter necessitated cash for Napoleon.

The Louisiana Purchase took place on April 30, 1903, in Paris, and the acquisition was finalized months later at the Cabildo in New Orleans. The cost was said to be eighty million francs or fifteen million dollars. Regardless of it being the largest land deal in history, New Englanders were not impressed. They did not care about Louisiana—or the West, for that matter. The sale nearly caused New Englanders to secede from the Union. President Thomas Jefferson appointed William Charles Cole Claiborne as governor, and Claiborne held that possession until after Louisiana was admitted to the union. The newly created territorial legislature established twelve subdivisions in the territory. They were Orleans, German Coast, Acadia, Lafourche, Iberville, Pointe Coupee, Concordia, Attakapas, Opelousas, Rapides, Natchitoches and Ouachita. Calling the subdivisions counties was confusing for the inhabitants, since most were familiar with parishes, given the fact that the majority were Catholics.

Despite the territory being composed of several nationalities, English was chosen as the language, which upset the inhabitants. Statehood would not be established until the population of the territory reached sixty thousand. The first newspaper established in New Orleans was *Le Moniteur de la Louisiane*, in 1794. The Odd Fellows Society, a fraternal order, established a lodge in Louisiana in 1831. Thirty years later, lodges were built in most larger towns. The Louisiana Historical Society was created in 1835 and reorganized in 1846. The most noted historian of the time was Charles E.A. Gayarre. He was also the most distinguished graduate of the College of Orleans at that time.

Gayarre later went to France and, in the French archives, he studied early history. Between 1846 and 1860, Gayarre published the *History of Louisiana* in four volumes, in French and English. He also wrote other great works about some of the most memorable people of Louisiana, including the biography of Judge François Xavier Martin. About 1830, the teaching of slaves to read was prohibited, especially after abolition literature began to be published. The distributors of such literature were called agitators, and they were severely dealt with. Night patrols of public roads were on the lookout for runaways and for the possibility of uprisings.

The first steamboat appeared on the Mississippi River in 1812. It was named *New Orleans* and cost $38,000 to build. It was 116 feet long and 20 feet across. In or about 1830, Louisiana had its first railroad. About thirty years later, New Orleans had three chartered rail lines. By 1840, New York and Baltimore were the only two U.S. cities larger than New Orleans. The first census of the Louisiana territory was taken in 1810, with a population of 76,550. Between 1822 and 1823, production of sugar was 30,000 hogsheads; each weighed 1,000 pounds. By 1860, that number was 221,726 hogsheads, generated by 762 plantations with a combined workforce of 50,670 slaves. The most valuable crop was corn, which was eaten by man and beast, and nearly every farm and planter grew it. But the money crop was cotton.

In 1870, James B. Eads was responsible for creating the system of jetties at the mouth of the Mississippi River. From 1903 to 1907, $3 million was spent building jetties at southwest pass. New Englanders were at it again; this time they were opposed to the Louisiana territory being admitted to the Union. U.S. Representative Josiah Quincy III of Boston, Massachusetts, led the resistance. He was against inclusion because he felt the territories boundaries were not clearly defined. And despite the French being in North America long before the English, Quincy's main bone of contention was that

Left to right: Author, Jack Winn of Lafayette and J.D. Soileau of Ville Platte examining historical documents at the Evangeline Parish public branch library in Ville Platte, Louisiana. *Photo courtesy of Francis Comeaux of Lafayette.*

the inhabitants of the territory had to be naturalized, which he said would take five years. Regardless of Josiah Quincy's disapproval, on February 11, 1811, Congress approved Louisiana joining the union on April 30, 1812. And so it was, on the ninth anniversary of the Louisiana Purchase, that Louisiana became the eighteenth state to join the union, after Ohio and before Indiana.

The state included the section between the Pearl River and the Mississippi River, which is still referred to as the West Florida Parishes. A legislative election was held, which resulted in William Claiborne becoming governor with thirty-three votes. His opponent, Jacques Villeré, received six votes. Thus, Claiborne became the first elected governor in the state of Louisiana. And as we know, Louisiana was admitted to the Union before the War between the United States and Great Britain. General Andrew Jackson fought the British along with a major force from Jean (John) and Pierre Lafitte and their crew of pirates and a group of frontiersmen with long rifles from Kentucky and Tennessee. McGinty argued that the British were using smooth-bore muskets that limited their range to perhaps one hundred yards, while the range of Andrew Jackson's riflemen was about three hundred yards. The reason for the difference was rifling, which put a spin on projectiles that increased accuracy and distance of the projectile. The riflemen were able to shoot down the British well before they got within firing distance of Jackson's men. British losses were 700 killed, about 1,400 wounded and 500 prisoners. Jackson's losses were 8 killed and 13 wounded. A peace treaty was acknowledged on December 24, 1814, between the United States and the British, two weeks before the Battle of New Orleans.

Sometime after 1818, the Good Roads Act implemented a provision for improving the section that the New Orleans to Nashville highway traversed, thus improving the U.S. Mail service. In 1823, a legislative decree enacted a provision for the construction of a new state penitentiary in Baton Rouge. Before the Baton Rouge penitentiary was built, until 1832, criminals were jailed in the penitentiary in New Orleans. After 1842, the public works department used Black convicts to construct levees and highways and to dredge bayous. Two years later, convicts were performing various manufacturing ventures inside the walls of the penitentiary for outside concerns. At that time, Louisiana's prison system was considered better than average. The Louisiana governor's salary was $6,000. The average salary of other state governors was $2,400 annually. Killing a man in a duel was made a capital offense. However, there is no written record of the law ever being assessed. In 1830, the state capital was moved to Donaldsonville "to

Author at book talk in the Young-Sanders Center in Franklin, Louisiana. *Photo courtesy of Jack Winn of Lafayette.*

remove State officials from insidious influences in the city." Two years later, Donaldsonville was said to be too small to accommodate all the activities associated with running a government, so the state capital was moved back to New Orleans. During that same period, Citizens Bank of New Orleans was chartered and began printing banknotes. On one side of the ten-dollar note was the French word *dix*, meaning "ten." Those notes circulated the country and soon became known as dixies; according to McGinty, that was how the South became known as Dixie Land.

The Panic of 1837 and the depression that soon followed caused the Louisiana government to imprison some of its citizens who were in financial straits. Back then, if you didn't pay your bills, you were sent to jail. At about that time, Louisiana had outside contractors to operate the state prison, and the contractors were given a grant to improve the prison, which was a substantial drain on the state. The law was repealed in 1840. Also in 1840, Alexandre Mouton of Vermilionville (Lafayette) became the first Democrat governor of Louisiana. He carried sixty percent of the votes. The following year, the Democrats elected all four of their state congressmen. Three years later, the undemocratic practice of the legislature selecting the governor and lieutenant governor was done away with.

Prior to ending this practice, the speaker of the house acted as lieutenant governor. The legislature voted on and approved a new constitution on the first Monday in November 1845. Citizens were no longer required to own property to vote. Voters had to reside in the parish for one year. Inhabitants had to wait two years after being naturalized to vote. You could only vote in the parish you resided in. Paupers, the insane, criminals and members of the United States military could not vote. Coroners, sheriffs and justices of the peace were elected. Judges of the supreme court had term limits of eight years. Lower-court judges were limited to six years. However, regular judges were appointed by the governor, as it was under the constitution of 1812. "All judges must be trained in the law and have practiced law in the state for five years." The legislature was to meet every other year, not to exceed sixty days, which was the maximum length of time they could meet. And the old law concerning duels was amended since it was not followed as written. The law now stipulated that any participant in a duel was disfranchised, which meant he could not vote. A clause was added that asked if an officer had participated in a duel since the new constitution was adopted—and if so, he probably forfeited his position.

The previous election law that allowed voters in the "rural districts" three days for voting was changed to permit one day. When addressing members of the legislature, French or English were acceptable. Both houses had interpreters, and the state's constitution and laws were written in French and English. However, "the secretary of state and the clerk of the house of representatives were both required to speak both languages." At that time, there were about forty parishes in the state. Some thought that was too many. Any new parish was required to be at least 625 square miles and contain five thousand citizens or more to ensure a representative in the house. The legislature proclaimed that the state capital was to be moved after 1848 and within sixty miles of New Orleans. As a result, it was moved to Baton Rouge.

The 1845 constitution made provisions for free public schools throughout the state. In 1848, the office of state superintendent of education was implemented, and Alexander Dimitry (1805–1883) was the first superintendent. A state seminary was to be established to promote "literature and the arts and sciences." Schools were mostly attended by boys, although girls did attend schools. The mindset back then was that "young women did not need higher learning; elementary education was sufficient." This was also the practice throughout the nation. The St. Charles College at Grand Coteau was established by the Jesuits of France. There was also the H. Sophie Newcomb

College for women, which was established in New Orleans in 1886. Leland University in New Orleans, a Baptist institution "for colored people," opened its doors in 1870. In 1920, it was moved to Baker, about twelve miles north of Baton Rouge. In 1898, Southwestern Louisiana Industrial Institute was established in Lafayette. And Grambling College, a state-supported college for Black people, began in 1901. An academy was fully functioning before the War Between the States: it was the Louisiana State Seminary of Learning and Military Institute, predecessor of LSU.

In 1852, Louisiana was not concerned with increasing talk of secession from the Union. It was primarily concerned with yellow fever, which had hit Louisiana hard, especially in 1853. Thousands of people died. Louisiana spent thousands of dollars in maintaining quarantine stations near the mouth of the Mississippi River. Until the twentieth century, the cause of the virus was unknown and there was no treatment. By 1860, the population of Louisiana was 708,002. There were 357,456 Whites, 18,820 free "colored" people and 331,726 slaves. On January 26, 1861, the delegates of the state convention voted for secession 113 to 17.

The War of Northern Aggression (the War Between the States) occurred between 1861 and 1865. We will not rewrite the stories of the war. However, the war did occur, and it reached Louisiana in 1862. After the war, Reconstruction lasted from 1865 to 1877, and according to most historians, it was far worse than the war itself. To really get a flavor of the war and Reconstruction, I highly recommend reading *The Southern Claims Commission* by Frank W. Klingberg, published in 1955. One of the best things to happen during the "Civil War": salt was found at Avery Island in Iberia Parish. Back then, "salt was quarried like stone." The Avery Island salt was said to be of such high quality that it "requires little or no processing." By 1876, the people of Louisiana had had their fill of Reconstruction. Judge Able of Louisiana alleged that "more money had been stolen from the state treasury by officials during the preceding eight years of carpetbag rule than by all the 'unofficial thieves, robbers and burglars since the time of the Louisiana Purchase.'"

Louisiana had a new constitution ratified and approved by the people on December 8, 1879. According to McGinty, the outcome of the general election was unanimous. "The entire Democratic state ticket was elected by large majorities, and the Democrats had overwhelming control of both houses of the legislature." In 1884, the Louisiana State Normal School for the training of teachers was constructed in Natchitoches, and Paul Tulane (1801–1887), an American philanthropist, donated more than $1 million to the University of Louisiana. "In appreciation of the gift, the name was changed to Tulane University of Louisiana."

In May 1890, the Louisiana legislature "enacted a law that required all railroads in the state to provide separate coaches [and waiting rooms] of equal comfort for white and colored passengers." The law also applied to steamships and other conveyances. It essentially required the railroad conductor or steamship captain to decide the race of each passenger. Before you judge Louisiana, it was not the only state to legislate such laws. That distinction also belonged to northerners. In fact, separate coaches were first established fifty-two years earlier in Boston. The year was 1838, and the railroad was the Eastern Railroad, along with other rail lines operating in Boston. Back then, some of the passengers in Boston called the colored coach the dirt car, while newspapers there referred to it as the Jim Crow coach.

Jim Crow was an ugly expression with racist connotations northerners liked to use most of the time when mentioning the racist South. Jim Crow, like the separate railroad passenger coaches, originated from and was first used in Boston. Again in 1838, Thomas Dartmouth Rice, a White northern entertainer, with the help of northern newspapers, coined the term "Jim Crow." It was part of Rice's comedy routine; according to him, he was the first White man to perform in blackface. Rice demonstrated his belief of what Black people looked and sounded like—idiots. "Jim Crow" soon made its way into New England's lexicon. "Boston merchants carried music boxes that played Jim Crow, Zip Coon, and other tunes." Apparently Northerners didn't think it was racist—not until after the War Between the States. There was even a dance called the Jim Crow Set that was popular in Kansas, Missouri and probably other states in the nineteenth century, according to David McCullough's 1992 book *Truman*, about Harry S. Truman, one of our greatest U.S. presidents. The Jim Crow Set was a popular dance in the mid-1850s, especially after a Kansas or Missouri frontiersman named James J. Chiles performed it enthusiastically. Chiles may have been a distant relative of the former president.

Another excellent book that I highly recommend reading is *Separate* by Steve Luxenberg. It's an eye-opener. For example, the 1896 *Plessy v. Ferguson* case, which took place in New Orleans, was staged. By that I mean it was planned in advance. It could have been staged in Boston, Philadelphia—or anywhere, for that matter. Why New Orleans? Why the South? Judge Albion W. Tourgee (1838–1905) later represented Homer Plessy in the United States Supreme Court battle. For Tourgee and most other northerners, the

War Between the States wasn't enough. The South had to pay. Tourgee and others thought the South had to "stay in territorial purgatory for a generation or more." And "the North, as a conqueror, was to rule the South, as a province for years to come." The editor of the *Alamance Gleaner*, a weekly newspaper based in Graham, North Carolina, wrote, "No reconciliation, no peace, no quiet, no freedom, no self-government for this generation, for the South." And that, my friends, is why Reconstruction lasted as long as it did.

One last thing about slavery: each year, we celebrate Columbus Day, which is said to represent our American heritage and the beginning of Western civilization. Who was responsible for starting the slave trade? According to Judge Napolitano, it was Christopher Columbus, when he returned to Spain from his first voyage to the New World. That was when he presented natives from Haiti to the Spanish royal court. It can be said that, more than anyone else, Columbus was the individual who began the evil institution of the slave trade in the United States.

I digressed a bit to explain the separate but equal legislation, which was neither separate nor equal. As an example, the passenger railcars, waiting rooms at railroad train depots and steamship compartments for Blacks were inferior to the spaces provided for Whites only. Now back to the history of Louisiana.

The charter for the Louisiana State Lottery expired in December 1893, and the following year, the Louisiana Industrial Institute at Ruston was chartered. The Duson brothers, Curly and Willie, from Crowley, Louisiana, along with the Southern Pacific Railroad, were instrumental in the land boom of the 1890s, which brought a multitude of folks from the Midwest, especially from Park and Union Counties of Indiana, who cultivated rice. The construction of the Southern Pacific Railroad provided rice growers easy access to markets. By the 1950s, 2,421 miles of irrigation canals were also helping the rice growers. In February 1889, the Louisiana legislature wrote another constitution to serve two purposes: it grandfathered in White voters (those who had legally voted in 1865), and it disfranchised Black people without violating the Fifteenth Amendment. The exclusion was upheld by the United States Supreme Court. In 1900, the Louisiana state prison lease system ended. From then on, prisoners worked under state supervision. Mortality among convicts decreased by nearly half. Within a decade, a penal farm was established, where convicts worked and produced their food. A home for people with leprosy (now known as Hansen's disease) was established by a $25,000 appropriation of state funds. And the magnolia was legally designated the state flower. In 1860, Louisiana had "eight daily, three semi-weekly, and seventy weekly newspapers, and two periodicals, with a combined annual circulation of 16,948,000 copies." And the *Times Picayune* was the only "pre-civil war newspaper to survive. It took over both, the *Times* and the *Democrat*."

In 1902, the first oil was discovered in the state, in the community of Evangeline, near Jennings, in the western part of Acadia Parish. Shortly thereafter, "oil was found at Welsh and Breaux Bridge" reported McGinty. The only sitting president of the United States to ever visit New Orleans did so on May 2, 1901, and that was President McKinley. In 1904, Louisiana established a state reform school for males under eighteen years of age, separating juvenile delinquents from savvy career criminals. In 1907, near the end of his term in office, Governor Blanchard stated that the worst handicaps facing the state were illiteracy and poor roads. His administration was credited with increasing or lengthening school terms by three months, which in effect increased the school term by 50 percent. Schools back then were in session for only three months. During Governor Sanders's administration, the first graveled highways were constructed. Sanders may have been the first, but the "Gravel Roads Governor" was John M. Parker. Prior to this, there were dirt roads. Most folks didn't dare drive on them after heavy rains.

In 1904, the Department of Forestry was created, which was the first step in protecting our lumber industry. Two years later, a law was created to limit "the size of trees to be cut." It was all for naught. The lumber industry reached its peak about 1920. Cypress and pine were the most abundant. In 1927, the great flood of that year was the most important issue concerning Louisiana and the country. It was by far the most destructive force to ever descend on the state.

Huey P. Long (1893–1935) became the fortieth governor of Louisiana in 1928. Love him or hate him, he did a lot toward building bridges and roads. He implemented the state's first highway system. Long built a few miles of concrete roads in each parish to give the residents a feel for what concrete was like over gravel. He also built a new state capital and governor's mansion costing $5 million and "a thirteen million dollar charity hospital in New Orleans." After his first term as governor, Huey was elected U.S. Senator Long. During that period, Louisiana's population reached 2,630,000. In 1935, while in the lobby of the state capitol in Baton Rouge, Long was assassinated by Dr. Carl Austin Weiss of Baton Rouge. Some say it was a conspiracy by Long's political enemies and Weiss drew the short straw. Others say Long was killed because of recent legislation that he had his legislature approve, which realigned Judge Pavy's voting district. Like every state in the Union, Louisiana back then had a two-party political system. However, it was untraditional. There were the pro-Longs and the anti-Longs, and—you guessed it—Judge Pavy was anti-Long. The legislation drastically changed Judge Pavy's political district, effectively killing his chance to be reelected. Judge Pavy was Dr. Carl Weiss's father-in-law. Yet others say it was Governor Long's bodyguards who accidently killed him. Today, Louisiana's population is 4.649 million.

Chapter 3

A MAN OF VISION

In 1898, Louisiana state senator Robert H. Martin (1853–1932) of Breaux Bridge authored, introduced and fought for the passage of Legislative Act 162, which called for the creation of an institution of higher learning in one of the parishes of the Thirteenth Legislative District of Louisiana. The tri-parishes of St. Martin, Iberia and Lafayette were all in Senator Martin's Thirteenth District, and they were all in the running for a new school of higher learning. Senator Robert Martin first introduced a bill in 1896 for a college in his Thirteenth District. Frank J. Patti, author of *The Life and Work of Edwin Lewis Stephens*, wrote in his dissertation and theses that the bill passed by one vote in the house and overwhelmingly passed the senate. Back then, there was not a college anywhere in southwest Louisiana. There was one in New Orleans, Baton Rouge, Natchitoches and Ruston. Governor Murphy Foster vetoed Senator Martin's bill due to lack of funds. Senator Martin gave it another try in 1898. This time, the bill passed by the house and the senate and was signed by Governor Foster.

On May 19, 1900, the *Lafayette Gazette* published an interesting article, "Gov. Foster's Message," which stated that earlier in the year, on January 3, a college planning and review board visited Lafayette and New Iberia to learn of the "inducements" offered by the proposed college locations. After reviewing the sites and, especially, learning of the inducements, the selection committee chose Lafayette. Here's what Lafayette offered:

> *First—the donation of twenty-five acres of land, beautifully situated, the gift of a private citizen* [Mrs. Maxim E. Girard and her son, Crow,

of Lafayette], valued at $2,500. Second—A cash bonus subscribed by the citizens of Lafayette of $5,000. Third—a cash bonus of the police jury of the parish of Lafayette, $3,000 and, Fourth—an annual tax of 2 mills [two hundredths of one dollar] *on the assessed valuation of the property of the parish of Lafayette for ten years.*

The article also reported that two banks in Lafayette immediately advanced the state $10,000 from the millage tax that had previously been voted on. Governor Foster concluded his statement with the following: "After considering the claims and qualifications of a number of educators, it was unanimously determined to place Prof. E.L. Stephens at the head of the institution, and he was accordingly duly elected and accepted the trust." Dr. Stephens was paid an annual salary of $1,500. Edwin L. Stephens was born on November 27, 1872, five years before the end of Reconstruction in Louisiana.

According to Patti, groundbreaking ceremonies for the "Main Building" (Martin Hall) at Southwestern Industrial Institute (SLII) began on Saturday, May 28, 1900, at a cost of $41,939. SLII opened its doors on September 18, 1991. As reported by Kathleen Thames, author of *100 Years: The University of Louisiana at Lafayette, 1900–2000*, when SLII was established, there were eight teachers: Dr. Stephens, who taught math; V.L. Roy, science; Ashby Woodson, manual training; Gertrude Mayfield, domestic science; Edith Garland Dupré, English and French; Florent Sontag, music; L.W. Mayer, stenography; and Beverly Randolph, drawing and gymnastics, who married Edwin L. Stephens ten months later. Enrollment for the opening year was 195 students. Cost for enrollment for Louisiana students was free. However, fees and other expenses were about $140 per year. The population of Lafayette Parish in 1900 was 3,314—which doubled a decade later.

Patti reported that when classes began at SLII, the requirement for students to take classes was the completion of the eighth grade, which created an upheaval. Shots were fired, windows were shattered and Sheriff Isaac "Ike" Broussard threatened to tear down the school in protest if the entrance standards weren't lowered. Stevens finally relented and allowed students to enroll after completing the sixth grade. During that era, most of the one- and two-room country schools went only as far as the sixth or seventh grade. Anything above seventh grade was considered higher learning. If anyone aspired to become a schoolteacher, they enrolled in what were called "normal" schools: e.g., the State Normal School in Natchitoches in northwest Louisiana. In conversations some years ago with Rodney Trahan, a former educator from Rayne, who is now deceased, he informed me that Gladys Amy and Olive Hartwell of Rayne High School became educators at the State Normal School in Natchitoches. Years later, state and parish education rules were changed, and both women were required to return to school for another course of study if they wanted to continue their employment. For several years, during the summer months, when SLII wasn't being utilized, it was used much like a normal school to teach educators.

Louisiana governor W.W. Heard presented diplomas to the first graduating class of SLII in 1903. Thames wrote that those eighteen graduates were Munger Ball, Annie T. Bell (valedictorian), Valsin Benoit, Maxime Beraud, Rhena Boudreaux, Mentor Chiasson, Ula Coronna, Harold Demanade, Jacques Domengeaux, Alma Gulley, Earl F. Hatfield, William P. Miller, Perry T. Singleton, Henry D. Smedes, D. Clarence Smith, Edith Trahan, Frederick Voorhies and Pothier J. Voorhies. On Monday, January 25, 1904, three years after the institution opened its doors, Stephens stood on the steps of the Main Building to honor Louisiana senator Robert Martin. On this momentous day, President Stephens was excited as a proud poppa when he announced the newly created two-year curriculum in telegraphy. He had good reason to be thrilled: this was the school's sixth course of study. His school was growing! In addition to the telegraphy announcement, Stephens was equally pleased to report the university had also recently built a new brick twenty-room girls' dormitory complete with a newly constructed cafeteria. The dorm "constitutes an altogether delightful, cultivated, and hospitable home," said Mrs. Elizabeth F. Baker, the dorm's matron. There were no dorms for the young men at SLII at that time. They were "comfortably placed with private families near the school grounds."

Despite being one of the youngest university presidents in the country at twenty-seven when hired, Stephens knew firsthand that telegraphers were vital components to railroading. In most cases, train dispatchers were located great distances from trains and railroad stations. Regardless of his age, Stephens hadn't always been a university president; years earlier, he was a railroader for the T&P (Texas & Pacific) railroad. He began his railroad career as a telegrapher at Provencal, which is in Natchitoches Parish near his hometown of Stephens Mill in northwest Louisiana. According to the same article, young Edwin L. Stephens also spent time as a telegrapher at Baton Rouge Junction (Addis) and later in Alexandria, and he had once been chief operator in the dispatcher's office of the Iowa Central Railroad at Marshalltown, Iowa. Patti's dissertation and theses mentioned that when Stephens first began work there, Superintendent

J.H. Redmon spoke highly of young Stephens and would introduce him as his adopted son.

Stephens could have been anything he set his mind to. Had he continued his employment with the T&P railroad, I am certain he would have joined the ranks of three other distinguished railroaders from Louisiana, one of whom was G.W.R. Baylcy of New Orleans, one of the premier charter members of the NOO&GW (New Orleans, Opelousas & Great Western) railroad. In 1852, Bayley directed the location survey party of the newly proposed railroad from New Orleans to Opelousas and later served as its chief engineer. He not only designed but also built many of the earlier bridges that spanned our waterways by rail between Algiers and Brashear City (Morgan City). He was also an impressive railroad cartographer and a resident engineer for James B. Eads, creator of the system of jetties at the mouth of the Mississippi River. He later became a Louisiana state legislator from 1875 to 1876, the year of his death. Next is Julius Kruttschnitt, also of New Orleans, who in the 1880s became vice president and general manager of the entire SPRR (Southern Pacific Railroad). Kruttschnitt was responsible for building much of Acadiana's railroad branch lines on Southern Pacific Railroad. And there was also Benjamin F. Biaggini, another native New Orleanian, who became president and CEO of Southern Pacific Railroad in 1964. Biaggini knew that for a company to be successful, it could not remain static; it either expanded with time or fell behind and faded away. Another fine SPRR (Southern Pacific Railroad) official on the former Lafayette Division was a superintendent who was fond of giving encouragement to his managers and supervisors. He would often say, "If you're not the lead dog, the scenery never changes."

In September 1889, Joseph Henry Stephens advised his son, Edwin, to return to school. Edwin Stephens enrolled at LSU while he held a job as night operator with the Texas Pacific Railroad at Addis, Louisiana. He graduated with a bachelor's degree from LSU on January 4, 1892. He also received the Faculty Medal, an achievement award for the student with the highest grade average during junior and senior year at LSU. According to Patti, by August 1892, Stephens was in Glens Falls, New York, where he had enrolled in education, which he completed in time to begin teaching at the State Normal College at Natchitoches for the school year 1892–93. Edwin boarded at the home of Thomas D. Boyd, president of the State Normal School. And in 1894, Edwin Stephens enrolled at Harvard University. He went on to become the only person in 1894 and probably beyond who met the qualifications for the Helen Gould Scholarship of $5,000 from the Texas

& Pacific Railroad. Helen was the daughter of Jay Gould, a railroad magnate and financial speculator when railroads were in their infancy.

Edwin graduated from New York University in June 1897 with a Master of Pedagogy and the following year graduated with a degree of Doctor of Pedagogy. In 1899, he returned to Louisiana, and as we know and greatly appreciate, Dr. Stephens was chosen as the first president of SLII. In 1904, when Edwin Stephens made his announcement in front of Martin Hall, the railroad had been in the Lafayette area for only a generation. American railroads had increased considerably in mileage and employment. The industry held promise for the growing community. It was quickly recognized that telegraph lines and railroad lines were a natural complement. Railroad station agents and telegraphers soon became one, which meant that the agents learned to be telegraphers. As the rail miles expanded, so did the need for agent/telegraph operators.

Edwin Stephens was a man of great foresight. He knew there should be a curriculum to teach telegraphy, and he knew who should teach it. Stephens could have easily taught the course himself. However, he chose General Manager Faye of SPRR, who was quick to oblige. Faye assigned a chief train dispatcher to teach the course. While maintaining his full-time employment, the chief dispatcher taught the course at SLII. Faye also made it clear there would be immediate job openings for the prospective new telegraph operators after their completion of the two-year course. You might be interested to know that Thomas Edison was once a telegraph operator. He enjoyed his work so much he called his first two sons (Marion and Thomas Jr.) Dot and Dash, a reference to Morse code.

Telegraphers had to be proficient with the telegraph key and the dot-dash code to copy train orders for train and engine crews. The dot-dash signals from the telegraph key created an audible signal at the other end of a telegraph line. It enabled the recipient or telegrapher to interpret and transcribe a message. Telegraphers reported the arrivals and departures of trains at their station. Accuracy was of the utmost importance. Lives depended on it, as did a reliable, railroad-approved pocket watch. The first and only head-on collision between two passenger trains in Louisiana occurred at Ricohoc in 1925, between Franklin and Patterson in St. Mary Parish. Mismanagement of train orders by one of the locomotive engine crews was determined to be the deadly cause.

Patti's work revealed that in 1903–4, the president's home at SLII was built near the main building at a cost of $3,999. That was the same year of the *Vermilion*, the school's twice-monthly news publication—created and run by students. Today, the publication is titled *La Louisiane*. In 1906, SLII began to expand. The state legislature purchased twenty-five acres of property next to SLII's existing twenty-five at a cost of $10,000. By 1907–8, students enrolling at SLII were required to have completed the first half of the seventh grade to take classes. In 1908, SLII's request to create its own normal school was finally approved. The handling of teacher certifications at SLII's normal school caused a rift between Stephens and T.H. Harris, who had recently been appointed Louisiana's state education superintendent. Harris felt that Stephens had overplayed his authority and wrote to him saying so. In Harris's opinion, Stephens would be fortunate if he kept his normal school after this incident.

In 1915–16, SLII added other courses of study, e.g., "Stenograph, Academic-Industrial Course," which was about bookkeeping and accounting. The entrance requirement was now "the completion of the 9th grade or the equivalent." The following year, SLII built a cattle barn that was one hundred feet long by forty feet wide and included twenty stalls. In 1918, SLII implemented a student army training corps, and on July 20, 1918, Lafayette Parish sustained its first war casualty from the war to end all wars. The young sixteen-year-old war hero was killed "over there" in Europe. His name was Louis Stanley Martin. The following February 22, 1919, Stephens planted a live oak in Stanley Martin's honor near the Main Building. It joined the other live oak trees that President Stephens had planted on January 1, 1901, near the Main Building. The Stanley oak is referred to as the guardian of the gate. Stanley Martin's body was sent home after the war and was buried in St. John's Cemetery on August 25, 1921, on his birthday. Lafayette American Legion Post 69 was named in his honor. As previously mentioned, the eighteen live oaks planted on January 1, 1901, are called century oaks because they were planted on the first day of the twentieth century, and according to UL's website, only ten remain.

By 1920–21, SLII had changed its name to SLI (Southwestern Louisiana Institute) and begun offering four-year courses that led to Bachelor of Arts degrees. Sometime in the 1930s, Stephens purchased an automobile. He liked to say it was a "Beau Nash," which was a reference to Robert "Beau" Nash, who was said to be an English leader of fashion during the eighteenth century. President Stephens and his wife made road trips on Le Vieille Trace Espanole (the Old Spanish Trail, or OST), which was probably what inspired Dr. Stephens to create the live oak society. Or perhaps it was after reading Walt Whitman's poem "I Saw in Louisiana a Live Oak Growing." Stephens believed the live oak should not have been named for any other state besides Louisiana. There is just no telling how many live oak trees Stephens and his wife counted along the OST during road trips to and from New Orleans. Stephens created the Louisiana Live Oak Association, composed of trees that were at least a century old. He listed forty-three trees as charter members, with the Locke Breaux live oak number one. Patti reported that the tree was owned by Samuel Locke Breaux of New Orleans, a descendant of John Locke (1632–1704), the English philosopher, who influenced our Declaration of Independence. Edwin Stephens wrote, "The constitution and by-laws of the society," and they were published on February 1, 1935.

In 1934, during the Great Depression, John Lomax, a pioneering American musicologist and folklorist, did much for the preservation of American folk songs. While traveling through Louisiana, John and his son Alan Lomax recorded a number of Cajun musicians. A surprising tidbit regarding SLII's first president came from John "Pudd" Sharp, assistant director of the research center for Louisiana studies at ULL, who informed me that Edwin L. Stephens was also recorded by Lomax on June 13, 1934. Stephens sang a Cajun French song a cappella. The song was "La-bas dans Carencro" ("Over There in Carencro"). His singing made it sound as though he was an authentic francophone, and given the period, it was certainly possible. French was predominantly spoken in Louisiana back then, and most places of business spoke Cajun French, especially in the Cajun triangle known as Acadiana. And since Edwin Stephens was from the Natchitoches area, it is highly probable he spoke French. Natchitoches was one of the original French settlements dating to the early 1700s. In addition to the Cajun French song, Stephens also sang a timeless hymn, "Crossing Over in Jordan," which he had learned from George Cooper of Florida, an old Black railroad gandy dancer (track laborer), while constructing the Texas and Pacific rail line in northwest Louisiana.

During the school session of 1937–38, SLI finally progressed from a middle-school-level institution to a full-fledged four-year college. On January 1, 1938, Edwin Stephens retired as president of the university. According to Patti's dissertation and theses, this "was not entirely voluntary." Perhaps it was because he and T.H. Harris didn't see eye to eye, which may have stemmed from when Harris was a student of Stephens while at the State Normal School. Or perhaps it was because of the numerous political figures in Lafayette that opposed Stephens. As mentioned earlier, Stephens and H.T. Harris were never best of friends. Prior to retirement, Stephens told an associate that he did not trust Harris. And as it was, Edwin Stephens retired. As Longfellow once said, "The wheels of justice turn slowly, but grind exceedingly fine." Two years later, after the 1940 election, T.H. Harris was replaced, and shortly thereafter, so was Lether Edward Frazar, the president of Southwestern Louisiana Institute.

When Stephens retired, he and his wife stayed at a cottage in Ocean Springs, Mississippi, and later moved to New Orleans. Ten months later, following a short illness, Stephens died at his home. The date was Saturday, November 5, 1938. Funeral services and the burial were in Natchitoches the following morning at eighty thirty. The pallbearers were all close friends: Dan Debaillon, T.M. Callahan, J.J. Davidson, Jr., H.L. Griffin, A.W. Bittle, Maurice Heyman and George G. Hughes, all of Lafayette, and Dr. James Monroe Smith of Baton Rouge. Stephens left a wife and three daughters.

Today, ULL, previously known as SLII, SLI and USL, now has more than "150 acres of land and over 2.1 million square feet of buildings" in Lafayette.

I DOFF MY HAT to the following for their assistance with this chapter: Dr. Bruce Turner (deceased), assistant dean of special collections; Mr. Al Bethard (deceased), head of microfilms at ULL; Ms. Jean Kinsell (retired); and Jane Vidrine (retired), of the Louisiana Room. I also thank Zachary Stein, head of special collections/assistant professor of library science at ULL; Christopher Bienvenu of the Louisiana Room; John Sharp, assistant director of the research center for Louisiana studies at ULL; Dr. Gary Howard, for his paper on live oak trees; and reference librarian Greg Lavergne of South Regional Library in Lafayette. I especially want to thank Frank J. Patti for his excellent work on the biography of Dr. Edwin L. Stephens.

Chapter 4
REBIRTH OF CAJUN MUSIC

Like those of many other bright young musicians, Iry LeJeune's life was cut short, and we're left to wonder what might have been. To put his music in perspective, by the time Loretta Lynn taped her first record in 1960 at age twenty-eight, Iry had already recorded all his music—twenty-six sides, one for every year of his life. He recorded two for the Opera label in Houston and twenty-four for Goldband Records in Lake Charles, Louisiana. Iry's unforgettable music and fame have grown over time. He is gone, but his music lives on. It is now legendary. Thanks to Iry's captivating music, he became an icon in Cajun music posthumously. It has been said countless times that he influenced more young Cajun musicians than any of his contemporaries. Iry LeJeune was not only an accomplished accordionist but also a talented singer-songwriter.

Gercie Daigle of Church Point grew up in Pointe Noir and knew Iry and his family well. Iry Joseph LeJeune was born to Agnus LeJeune and Lucie Bellard on October 28, 1928. This was Iry's mother's second marriage. In her first marriage, she had one child, who was visually impaired. From her second marriage, Iry was the oldest of four kids—he and a sister had vision problems and were considered legally blind, which was probably an inherited trait. Iry's parents were sharecroppers who eked out a living by growing cotton in the mysterious community of Pointe Noir. The area is near Pointe de l'Eglise or Church Point in the northeastern corner of Acadia Parish. Because of the many musicians from there, *c'est le nique de musiciens* (it's the epicenter or birthplace of Cajun musicians).

Alpha Bergeron, excellent accordion player of Pointe Noir. After World War II, Alpha played music seven nights a week. Alpha's son was the legendary singer and steel guitar player Shirley Ray Bergeron. *Photo courtesy of Gercie Daigle of Church Point.*

Due to Iry's near total blindness, his Uncle Angelas "Nonc Jack" LeJeune, one of the best accordion players of his time, allowed his nephew to "practice" with his accordion while the family toiled the fields. Iry loved music, especially the old style played by Amédé Ardoin. Music was his only form of entertainment. Gercie Daigle said Iry attended a school for the blind, which was located in Baton Rouge. Jack Daigle, a prominent businessman from Church Point, arranged to have Iry brought to school in the fall and returned to take him home in the summer. While at school, Iry learned to play the violin, but he preferred his accordion. It's been said that Iry played old-style accordion and sang from the heart.

Mike Leadbetter, editor of *Blues Unlimited* magazine of London, wrote a lengthy article in January 1968 about Iry LeJeune. At the time, Leadbetter was the world's foremost authority on postwar blues. He titled his article "Iry LeJeune—The Legend," and as Leadbetter wrote in his article, he had visited Louisiana specifically "for the many conflicting stories about his [Iry

LeJeune's] age and his music, and I was very curious to find out just what did happen during his short life." Leadbetter wrote of staying in Church Point when Shirley Ray Bergeron offered to have him meet Iry's family. Leadbetter asked questions in English, Agnus (Iry LeJeune's father) answered in French and Bergeron interpreted for the two.

After World War I, into the 1920s and through the early 1940s, the accordion was pushed aside while string bands were all the rage. According to Leadbetter, "It was the string band era of Cajun music. Happy Fats, Leo Soileau, Harry Choates, and the Hackberry Ramblers were the stars." In 1948, Iry begged Floyd LeBlanc, a friend, to take him to Houston to record on the Opera label. When Iry recorded "La Valse du Pont D'Amour (Love Bridge Waltz)," that was when everything began to fall into place, not only for Iry but also for Cajun music in general. Leadbetter said, "That record was a big seller and for the first time in ten years, the accordion wailed from the jukeboxes!" That was truly a watershed moment for Cajun music and for Cajun culture in every sense of the word. As we now know, there is plenty of room for both the fiddle and the accordion. Iry LeJeune recorded twenty-six sides at Goldband Records from 1947 until the very peak of his career. At that time, Iry was in his early twenties and rightly credited for the rebirth of Cajun music. "When they couldn't get Iry, [the] public's appreciation of Iry LeJeune's talent grew quickly." No doubt Leadbetter was moved not only by the eccentric music but also by the hardships, compassion, boldness and determination of Iry's short lifespan.

Steven LeJeune was an accomplished accordion player and an uncle of Iry LeJeune. On March 22, 1977, he was interviewed by Dr. Barry Ancelet, who at the time was a folklorist and professor at USL, the local university in Lafayette (now UL). I might add that the interview was entirely in Cajun French. Steven LeJeune said he would correct his nephew at times when

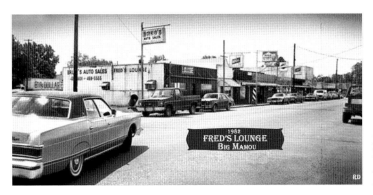

Fred's Lounge of Mamou, Louisiana. *Photo courtesy of Richard DesHotels.*

Iry first began playing the accordion at age ten. "Iry got nervous and at times played too fast, and sometimes forgot the lyrics or mixed them with other songs." It obviously takes a great deal of *envie* (determination) and time to master the accordion. Perhaps a decade or more ago, on an early Saturday morning, I was at one of Mark Savoy's jam sessions near Eunice. Savoy, one of the most renowned accordion players and accordion builders, suggested to aspiring accordion players to first listen carefully to a song at least one thousand times before picking up the accordion. Iry's Nonc Steven remembered when Iry first began playing house dances. "He was 13 years of age and by 17, Iry was playing professionally." Iry played the accordion with great excitement and sang with equally great emotion. It was sort of "a wailing or crying style" Iry had developed, said his uncle.

Stewart McBride, staff correspondent for the *Christian Science Monitor*, wrote a full-page article in the *Journal Tribune* dated August 25, 1982, titled "Louisiana's Cajun." The article was about Iry LeJeune and Cajuns in general. His source was none other than Barry Ancelet. Iry was well known at local dance halls, but that was as far as it got in the early 1940s. His popularity was limited due to the two previous decades when the fiddle cast a long shadow over the accordion, which was forced to take a backseat to the fiddle. McBride quoted Ancelet, who said, "After World War I, Cajun music began to lose its distinctive flavor. You could hear the Americanization process going on in the '20s and '30s." The death knell for the accordion was the string bands and Western swing era. "By the late '30s musicians who barely spoke English, were trying to sing in English," said Ancelet with a touch of humor. Iry's hit song "La Branche du Murier (The Mulberry Branch)" was what did it, confirmed Ancelet. "Nobody had yelled like that in ten years. He [Iry LeJeune] was taking his finger out of the dike and that song was the pivot that all Cajun music turned around on," beamed Ancelet.

St. Landry Homestead Federal Savings Bank of Eunice, on March 20, 1989, perhaps as a courtesy, had Melony LeMay transcribe a brief summary of Eddie Shuler and Iry LeJeune's early years of recording music together. In 1948, after staying several months in Houston, Iry recorded two hit songs, "Love Bridge Waltz" and "Evangeline Special." Afterward, Iry returned home, and at KPLC radio in Lake Charles, Louisiana, he met Eddie Shuler, who at the time was a young pioneering recording engineer. Shuler took a chance on Iry when no one else would. With only a handshake as their sacred bond, Iry and Shuler agreed to a recording contract. According to Leadbetter, Iry recorded "The Calcasieu Waltz" and "Teche Special," which further enhanced Iry's recording career. Accordions were now the hottest

Leleux's Dancehall south of Crowley, Louisiana. It was a combination grocery, dance hall and hardware store. The young men's section *et les vieux garçons* was dubbed "*la cage aux chiens*" by retired Professor Barry Ancelet. This photo was taken in 1938 during the height of the Great Depression by the now-famous photographer Russell Lee of the Farm Securities Administration. *Courtesy of the Library of Congress.*

musical instruments around. "Nathan Abshire hit the bigtime, followed closely behind by Lawrence Walker," with his trademark white shirt and black tie.

At Dupré Library in Lafayette, there is a treasure trove of audio and video recordings from early shows of the Liberty Theater in Eunice thanks to Jerry Devillier, their videographer, and John "Pudd' Sharp, who at the time was assistant director for research at the Center for Louisiana Studies at UL. Many of those recordings are of Ancelet interviewing various musicians, family members and others who personally knew Iry. Ancelet is the preeminent expert on Cajun music. Among the hundreds of audio recordings at Dupré Library, there is one of Eddie Shuler, who recorded some of Iry's music using a portable tape recorder, which was relatively new at that time. According to Shuler, the "Durald Waltz" was recorded at Iry's home in Lacassine; a dog's bark can clearly be heard in the recording. Shuler said that Iry debated whether or not he would play the fiddle while singing. After careful consideration, Iry sang, while Wilson "Pill" Granger, who might have been a more accomplished fiddler, played the fiddle. According to the audio recording of Shuler, the "Durald Waltz" was an original—someone whistled the tune while Iry wrote the lyrics. Incidentally, that waltz is the only recording by Iry LeJeune where the accordion was not featured. Shuler also said that after playing dances, Iry usually purchased a bag full of hamburgers for his family, who always stayed up waiting for his return. It saddens me to think of those poor innocent children waiting for their father on the night of October 8, 1955, when Iry was tragically killed.

The *Ottuma Courier* of June 26, 2016, reported in Selections for Library of Congress' 2009 National Music Registry that in order to make the national selection, the music had to be at least ten years old and be "culturally,

John Leleux, son of the great fiddler and luthier Lionel Leleux. John in his own right is an accomplished musician. He played guitar for the legendary Joe Falcon of Rayne. *Photo courtesy of John Leleux of Crowley.*

historically or aesthetically significant." Iry LeJeune's "Evangeline Special" and "Love Bridge Waltz," recorded in 1948, made the cut, along with Loretta Lynn's "Coal Miner's Daughter" (1970) and Willie Nelson's "Red Headed Stranger" (1975). Imagine that! More importantly, imagine if Iry had lived beyond his twenty-six years. Unfortunately for us, and Cajun music, Iry LeJeune died during the peak of his career—1955. Undeniably, Iry's music is now considered classic, and it can be heard in any dance hall throughout Acadiana and in many venues around the world. The book *Dancehalls of Cajun Country*, created in 2014 and maintained by John "Pudd" Sharp of Lafayette, reports that Jean Batiste "JB" Fuselier was driving while Iry was his passenger after they played a dance at the Green Wing Club in Eunice. "JB's automobile had a flat tire about five miles west of Eunice along LA Hwy 190." While JB was replacing the flat tire, an automobile crashed into them. Fuselier was seriously injured and eventually recovered, but Iry was knocked some distance from the roadway and died there. According to *Cajun Music, a Reflection of a People* (vol. 1), written by Ann Savoy and published in 1984, the driver that ran into their automobile was Luther Holt of Houston. Iry's old man voice trapped in a young man's body was taken from us just nineteen days shy of his twenty-seventh birthday. Thankfully, he and his music are immortalized. Many musicians, young and old, say they were heavily influenced by the music of Iry LeJeune. Cajun music is stronger today than ever before, thanks to Iry.

Nathan Abshire, the legendary accordion player, was the eldest of six children born on June 27, 1913, in the community of Riceville, just south of Bayou Queue de Tortue, the boundary separating Acadia and Vermilion Parish. According to *Tears, Love, and Laughter* by Pierre Varmon Daigle, published in 1972, several members of Nathan's family played the accordion, including his mother and father. Nathan began playing by age six and was playing at *bals de maison* (house dances) by eight. In the 1930s, Nathan would often walk to the community of Leleux, ten miles south of

The world-famous Fred's Lounge of Mamou, Louisiana. *Photo courtesy of Richard DesHotels.*

Crowley, to play music with Lionel Leleux at Ernest Leleux's dance hall—Lionel's father's dance hall. It was a grocery store, hardware store, blacksmith shop and dance hall combination situated about one mile south of Bayou Queue de Tortue where a person could buy almost anything they might need. It was on the right-hand side of the traveled road going south on what became Louisiana Highway 13. There were plenty of dance halls back then. According to Lionel's son John Leleux of Crowley, "There was one about one mile before [north] of the above-named bayou on the right owned by a Mr. Istre. Another dance hall owned by a Mr. Herpin was located about three miles south of Leleux's dance hall on the left."

There are a couple of great black-and-white photos of a seating section inside Leleux's dance hall affectionately called *la cage aux chiens* (the dog cage) by UL professor Barry Ancelet (now retired). The photos were taken in 1938 by the now-famous photographer Russell Lee. The photos are from the collection of the Farm Securities Administration, which consists of nearly two thousand photos taken during the Great Depression. It was part of the WPA (Works Progress Administration) project. It was part of the New Deal agency created by President Franklin Delano Roosevelt. Russell Lee was one of many photographers across the country documenting American cultures during that era. As stated by John Leleux, some of the young men shown in the photo on page 56 were actually sitting on funeral caskets. The gentleman on the left side seated with the hat is reported to be Célia Adams from the Leleux community. The young man wearing the white shirt sitting to the right of and behind Adams is Dan Leleux, Lionel's youngest brother.

As mentioned elsewhere, Nathan Abshire and Iry LeJeune are credited with the rebirth of Cajun music after the Second World War. It all began, according to Barry Ancelet, after our military heroes from World War II began returning home. "The returning war veterans wanted to hear the music they grew up hearing before the accordion was pushed aside and no longer featured on recordings." Nathan was part of that generation that served during World War II. After serving a stint in the army, he played regularly at the Avalon Club in Basile, which became his adopted hometown. In 1949, Nathan recorded his renowned "Pine Grove Blues," and as Varmon Daigle said, after that record, Nathan's career "took a leap." Varmon thought Nathan was "one of the most versatile and interesting Cajun musicians who ever lived."

Barry Ancelet said Nathan was like a metronome—every note and tempo was delivered on time, every time, never too fast, nor too slow. In 1976, Nathan performed with other well-known Cajun musicians at the Smithsonian Festival of American Folklife, which I understand is the largest annual cultural event in Washington, D.C. An excellent performance viewed by thousands was followed by an outpouring of applause. This was something Nathan and other Cajun musicians from the Acadian triangle weren't accustomed to hearing. There were countless autograph seekers wanting Nathan's autograph after his performance. Much to the dismay of the music fans, Nathan politely declined their requests. This left the impression that Nathan didn't care about his fans. Nothing could be further from the truth. Although Nathan was an excellent singer and music composer, he never learned to read or write. Nathan couldn't sign his name if his life depended on it, which was not only frustrating for him—it was also humiliating. Nathan spoke Cajun French and struggled to speak English. At the time, Barry Ancelet was not yet a faculty member at USL—not until the following year, 1977. Ancelet was at the folklife festival as a presenter with the group from Louisiana. Nathan informed Ancelet about the autograph-signing incident. Within a matter of minutes, using stick figure letters, Ancelet had Nathan signing his now-famous trademark signature. From that moment on, "N A" was Nathan's signature, including on all legal documents.

Another unfortunate incident occurred while at the folklife festival—one so disturbing to Nathan that he was ready to call it quits and return home. Ancelet was once again called to action. Nathan was uncertain as to which restroom door to open. Ancelet explained to Nathan that he should enter the restroom through the door with the shortest name: for instance, "Men" instead of the longer word "Women." Nathan explained that he had once gone into a restroom with the shortest name on the door, but instead of the usual "Men" or "Women" on the door, the signs read "Ladies" and "Gentlemen." Despite the two unfortunate incidents, Nathan had a good time, which could have been the origin of his legendary slogan: "The good times are killing me!" Like most Cajun musicians, Nathan made money playing music; however, it didn't adequately provide for his family. In order to supplement his income, Nathan worked a day job as overseer of the Basile town dump. Unfortunately, too much good times and alcohol coupled with poor health took its toll. Nathan Abshire died on May 13, 1981, just two weeks shy of his sixty-ninth birthday. He wanted his music buried with him. Fortunately, that request was denied. Although Nathan could not read or write, he left his mark on Earth. His music lives on and is in every Cajun musician's repertoire. His music can be heard in any number of dance halls throughout Acadiana.

I mentioned earlier the talented Pierre Varmon Daigle from Pointe Noir, who wrote a number of great books not only on the plight of the Acadians but also on Cajun musicians. Besides that, Varmon wrote all the lyrics and the music arrangements for the band Cajun Gold featuring Paul Daigle and Robert Elkins—both great artists. On April 13, 2022, I interviewed Robert Elkins at his home. I also interviewed his wife, Vicki, and their son Josh, who is a musical prodigy. He plays any instrument he puts in his hands, including the accordion and the fiddle. I felt blessed to sit in Robert's memorabilia room from his days of playing music. Hands down, Robert's singing voice was so clear, precise and instantly recognizable.

Varmon used many old phrases that he had heard and collected over the years from an old grocery store merchant in Church Point. His are some of the most beautiful Cajun songs you will ever hear. I was especially pleased to sit at the same round table where the lyrics and musical arrangements were created for Cajun Gold. One of my all-time favorite songs crafted by Varmon is "J'aime mieux t'avoir perdu" ("I'd Rather Have Lost You Than to Never Have Known You") featuring Paul Daigle and Robert Elkins. When Cajun Gold's album was recorded in 2000, it quickly gave other musicians new music to add to their repertoire. Unfortunately, Pierre Varmon Daigle died one year after the album was released. Daigle was seventy-seven years old—much too young to die. He had plenty more songs to write.

Robert Elkins and his son Josh Elkins sitting at the table where Pierre Varmon Daigle composed, arranged and organized his music. Varmon's musicians always said you played the music the way he wanted it played, or you weren't going to play it at all. *Author's collection.*

One of the first Acadian groups to perform at a National Folklife festival did so in Dallas in 1936, according to *Cajun Sketches*, written by Lauren C. Post in 1962. Post was a native of Rayne, Louisiana, and was the chairman that year for the Louisiana section going to perform in Dallas. Musicians from southwest Louisiana who performed in Dallas were "Lawrence Walker, accordion player; Aldus Broussard, fiddler; Sidney Broussard, fiddler; Junior Broussard, guitar player; Norris Mire, guitar player; and Evelyn Broussard, triangle player and singer." Post went on and mentioned the following singers: Lawrence Walker, Aldus Broussard and Elmer Sonnier, who was said to be "an educated and trained Cajun singer from Scott." He was a special soloist. Alan Lomax, an authority on folk music, commented that "Aldus [Broussard] was the best example of folk talent in the whole festival." Post mentioned that the most knowledgeable person regarding Acadian folk songs during that era was Irène Whitfield Holmes of Lafayette. While at LSU, she wrote her master's thesis, titled *Louisiana French Folksongs*, which was published by University Press in 1939. I digressed a bit to tell you about Lauren C. Post and Irène Whitfield Holmes; now, back to the rebirth of Cajun music.

I would be negligent if I didn't mention Lafayette's first folklife-type festival, spearheaded by Barry Ancelet and Dewey Balfa. The event took place at Blackham Coliseum on March 26, 1974, for a packed audience. The event was titled A Tribute to Cajun Music, Hommage à la Musique Acadienne. The performers were the Balfa brothers, Clifton Chenier, Alphonse "Boissec" Ardoin, Nathan Abshire, Jimmy C. Newman, Rufus Thibodeaux, Merlin Fontenot, S.D. Courville, Dennis McGee, Inez Cataton, Blackie Forestier, Lionel Leleux, Mark Savoy, Dieu Donné "Don" Montoucet of Scott and Varise Conner of Lake Arthur. Varise Conner and Lionel Leleux could play with the best during their time.

Varise Conner was not well known to the public unless you were from Lake Arthur. He is often referred to as the "greatest unrecorded Cajun musician." Conner was a lumberjack by trade and had his own sawmill at his home, which is where he was interviewed by Barry Ancelet and Michael Doucet between 1975 and 1977. The following is from Varise Conner's conversations and music recordings, along with personal conversations with Mitch Conner, Varise's youngest son. Varise's recordings are available through the Archives of Cajun and Creole Folklore at ULL. Between most songs, Varise Conner is heard speaking French and in English in his strong Cajun French accent. When Ancelet first met Varise Conner, he felt that because of Conner's profession and rough-hewn size, he could not possibly

Varise Conner was an exceptional fiddle player from a long line of fine fiddlers. *Photo courtesy of Mitch Conner, youngest of Varise's seven children.*

play such a delicate instrument as the violin. He was astonished when Conner's large hands produced such beautiful music.

Ancelet said Varise Conner was a humble man, not showy or flashy. All he wanted to do was play his music. On his recordings, Varise played Cajun French waltzes and two-steps, as well as polkas, mazurkas, blues, country and swing-type music. They were nearly all high-energy dance tunes: e.g., "St. Louis Blues," "You've Got to See Your Mama Ev'ry Night or You Won't See Your Mamma at All" and "Old South." During the interview with Ancelet and Doucet, Varise was accompanied by Andy Benoit, his stepson, who suffered from a heart ailment at the time. Varise learned the above tunes from Hubert Fontenot, an old-time fiddle player. Unfortunately, Fontenot is not listed in Ann Savoy's excellent book *A Reflection of a People*, which is my go-to book when looking for a certain Cajun French song or musician. Hubert Fontenot's music was played during the era before the accordion was made popular.

Although Varise Conner's ancestors came from Ireland in the mid-1800s, they were 100 percent Cajun. Varise Conner was born in 1906 to parents Arsen and Emma (Granger) Conner. Varise Conner's father, Arsen, and grandfather Octave Conner all played the fiddle, including his uncles and cousins, at *bals de maison* (house dances) and at family gatherings in and around Lake Arthur. Varise learned to play the musical instrument from his father beginning at the age of twelve on a twelve-dollar secondhand fiddle bought *par associé* (between he and his father.) They purchased it from a cousin named Adelard Conner. Varise's older brother Valsin played the base fiddle, while his youngest brother, Murphy, played the guitar. They played mostly for friends and relatives, and Varise played with a few bands early on. However, due to economic hardship during the Great Depression, even though admission to a dance hall cost very little, most folks didn't have the money. Large crowds gathered outside for a chance to hear the music. This was probably heartbreaking for Varise. According to Mitch Conner, Varise convinced the owner to let the people in even though they didn't pay admission. No one made money that day. Varise gave up playing his violin at about that time (1935) and didn't pick it up again until 1956 after his daughter Ethyl encouraged him to play for family and friends, which is what he did. Varise Conner died on June 19, 1994.

Varise Conner playing music with friends. He enjoyed doing house dances. *Photo courtesy of Mitch Conner.*

The multitalented Courtney Granger, a grandson of the late Dewey Balfa. Like his grandfather, Courtney was a talented Cajun fiddler and singer. Both were taken from us too soon. *Photo courtesy of David Simpson and cajunzydecophotos.com.*

In an email exchange, the excellent fiddle player David Greely informed me that on September 19, 2004, the Festivals Acadiens et Creoles was dedicated to Varise Conner. Greely also informed me that years ago, numerous field recordings of different musicians were forgotten and abandoned in a small room at the archives of ULL. Fortunately, they were found, along with "shelves full of field recordings, including the ones Barry [Ancelet] made of Varise in the '70s." For two years, while renovations at Dupré Library were taking place, the old tapes were subjected to heat and humidity. Greely took the tapes to an archival specialist in New Orleans who digitized the recordings. After going through nine hours of Varise's early field recordings, Todd Mouton, John Laudun and Barry Ancelet decided to release an album from that assortment. Ancelet and Greely met sometime later and edited the recordings, focusing on capturing Varise's spoken words. An amazing collection of music on CD was produced by the Center for Louisiana Studies on the Louisiana Folk Masters record label. Greely also mentioned how well he was treated by Varise's sons, Mitch and Milton Conner. Varise's music is some of my all-time favorite music. In Acadiana, we are truly blessed to have such a great number of Cajun musicians.

I enjoy great traditional Cajun music. There are too many of my favorites to name. I will say this: there are two Cajun musicians that I think sound more like Iry LeJeune than anyone else. They are Joel Sonnier and the late Courtney Granger (1982–2021). They have/had that old man's voice trapped inside a young man's body.

Chapter 5

LOST COMMUNITIES
OF THE BASIN

It seems the Atchafalaya basin has always been inhabited by Cajuns, and they have always been protective of this area. Kenneth Delcambre, author of *Lords of the Basin*, published in 1988, said the water table often fluctuated and had a direct effect on fish catches. He also reported that "as early as the 1870s, the unwritten laws of the basin were verbally spoken and understood. Many murders took place in their defense, and in the 1920s, maximum efforts were again enforced." Delcambre was referring to the hunting and fishing boundaries in the swamp. He reported, "At times they [Cajuns] were challenged by outsiders. And when they were, in many cases...in self-defense, they were shot on the spot, and the Cajuns would put hoop net weights on the victims and sent to the bottom of the Atchafalaya River." The area was never heavily populated. However, in 1900, that began to change. The railroad attracted people to the area, and unfortunately, it was the railroad that drove them away. Well, not entirely. Mother Nature played a big role.

The Southern Pacific Railroad (SPRR) put the communities of Atchafalaya, Pelba and others on the map. They were railroad stations between Baton Rouge and Lafayette. The rail line was referred to as the BR branch. Hundreds of workmen toiled to build the line. In the beginning of the railroad building, the railroad hired many locals and built housing for the construction crews. During the beginning of construction, wooden pilings were hammered and tracks were laid on top of them along with girders and stringers. In shallow water or marshy areas, railroad tracks were built, and dirt and shell were used as fill material. Delcambre reported that trainloads of dirt were hauled from Larrabie Pit to build a permanent embankment. The pit is on the east side of Lafayette along the Breaux Bridge highway. Railroad train crews kept the inhabitants of the basin supplied with necessities from the outside world. As time progressed, so did the communities. In 1908, the railroad line was finally put in operation. Delcambre reported that the rail line was a "most peculiar construction" and crossing it was said to be "unique." It was two-thirds bridge, one-third embankment.

The line was 57.4 miles long with the majority of it built on wooden pilings. A turn span opening for allowing the passage of watercraft at the Atchafalaya River was 232 feet. The depth of the river at the steel bridge structure opening was 100 feet. Back then, eastbound trains leaving Lafayette entered the branch line at BR Junction. Other stations were at Anse la Butte, Breaux Bridge, Nina, Henderson, Pelba, Atchafalaya River, Crusel, DesGlaise, Ramah, Gross Tete, Wilbert, Ithra and Anchorage at the eastern end. Delcambre wrote that trains crossed the Mississippi River by ferryboat and continued to downtown Baton Rouge where the line met the Yazoo and Mississippi Valley Railroad. The levee along the Atchafalaya back then was insufficient: "some places one could jump over the levees." According to Delcambre, sometime around 1915, an attempt was made to use prisoners to build state-mandated levees. It didn't work out as intended, so in 1919, the Corps of Engineers took on the task of building levees in the swamp. At that time, there were approximately 200 people living in the Atchafalaya swamp near the railroad line.

Delcambre reported that between 1914 and 1915, the area saw "a great increase in the economic importance of the fishing industry, which brought as much as $250,000 in a good year." During the First World War, entire trains of petroleum products for the war effort left Baton Rouge for all points west. Delcambre wrote of an incident in which a German sign painter working in the swamp was suspected of being a spy. The young man was apparently keeping tabs on the movements of trains, especially trains carrying petroleum. Authorities arrested the man, and he was never heard from or seen again. No one remembered his name.

Southern Pacific's 1922 timetable for the BR branch line indicated the maximum speed for passenger trains was 50 miles per hour and 35 for freight trains. However, when operating on the BR, trains were not to exceed 30 miles per hour between mile post 20 at the Atchafalaya River and mile post 29, east of Des Glaise. This was probably due to bridges for watercraft at those locations. Passenger train no. 705 left Baton Rouge at 6:40 a.m. and

Top: Atchafalaya post office. *Bottom*: Mr. Tom Bernard owned several businesses in the basin. *Photos courtesy of René Prejean.*

arrived in Lafayette at 10:05 a.m., and passenger train no. 710 left Lafayette at 1:35 p.m. and arrived in Baton Rouge at 5:00 p.m. There were several sidings between Lafayette and Baton Rouge; most were fifty or sixty railcar lengths long. Sidings are used for meeting or passing trains. A couple of the stations had a telephone and water available for steam locomotives. Today's sidings are constructed with heavier rails and crossties and are much longer than those of earlier times, and they're measured in miles and feet.

According to Division Engineer C.R. Shaw by way of Delcambre, "The line was always in the red—it never made a profit." During SP's two decades of operation, it spent "between five and six million dollars on maintenance alone. It was 48 miles of trestles," said Shaw. Shaw and other railroaders said the line should never have been built. Bridges constructed on wooden pilings in water are weak links in the rail system, and jointed rails make them even more susceptible to deterioration. Jointed rails are usually thirty-nine feet long, as opposed to continuous welded rails, nearly quarter-mile-long strings of rail welded together, which eliminate the pounding at rail ends that often causes a variety of track defects. All throughout the BR's existence, it was plagued with high water in the basin. Delcambre reported that in a 1972 interview, Sidney Martin, the SP Lafayette Division bridge and building supervisor for many of the early years, recalled, "When water covered the tracks, someone had to walk ahead of the engine to assure the engineer the tracks were in place, keeping in mind…this train carried passengers."

According to an interesting article by Daniel Hubbell during the heyday of the BR branch line, SPRR (Southern Pacific Railroad) was using a two-track ferryboat to cross the Mississippi River between Anchorage and Baton Rouge. Keep in mind that trains back then were not nearly as long as they are today. The ferryboat had a capacity of only sixteen freight railcars or eight passenger railcars, which was insufficient. So, in May 1922, George Herbert Walker, a savvy businessman from St. Louis who also happened to be the chairman of the board of the Gulf Coast Lines, which included Southern Pacific's Atchafalaya Branch line, worked out a deal with a ferryboat builder and purchased "a 340-foot sidewheeler with three tracks." The ferryboat was named after the railroad chairman. It was also the namesake of two future U.S. presidents, George Herbert Walker Bush and George Walker Bush, or "Dubya," as he was known. This ferryboat had more than adequate space to accommodate SP's trains coming off or going on the BR line. By 1923, the ferry was plying the waters of the Mississippi River, transferring SP's BR branch trains from Anchorage to Baton Rouge and vice versa. The price tag for the ferryboat was $250,000. That would be $3.5 million today. At about that time, there was talk about building a bridge to cross the Mississippi River for automobiles and train traffic. But for the time being, it was just a dream on the horizon. A few decades later, the dream came to fruition. However, when it came time to begin utilizing the bridge, railroad union members refused to do so until the ferryboat crews were properly compensated because they were losing their employment. As Hubbell described it, a disagreement ensued

Who says it doesn't snow in Louisiana? It rarely snows in south Louisiana, perhaps once every other decade. *Photo courtesy of René Prejean.*

that lasted a few weeks before it was finally settled and the boatmen were appropriately paid.

Besides a train depot in the community of Atchafalaya, or "Chaf," as it was referred to, there was a bakery, a post office, a fish market, a church, an ice factory and an apiary business owned by Tom Bernard, who "owned almost 90% of all the land that was once called Atchafalaya." Delcambre reported that "in 1905, public schools were initiated in St. Martin Parish." A one-room schoolhouse was built at Atchafalaya, which is in St. Martin Parish. A boat was used to take the children to school. The year is uncertain; however, the first schoolteacher at Atchafalaya was Elvina Aucoin Westfall. Her husband owned a grocery store at Atchafalaya. Unfortunately, in 1933, when her husband, George Westfall, died, Elvina moved to Krotz Springs and opened a hotel. The following year, Rona Resweber replaced Elvina as the schoolteacher. The author reported that in 1934, Beatrice Champagne Landry taught school at "Chaf." Nursey Herbert of Breaux Bridge also taught there.

In 1926, the weather service began making dire flood predictions for many states, including Louisiana. Southern Pacific Railroad took those predictions seriously. In early 1927, it began sending loaded barges of large boulders to the Atchafalaya bridge. Delcambre reported that by mid-May 1927, "water levels in the basin were extremely high"; trains ceased to run. An attempt to hold the steel structure in place began. "Cranes placed the huge boulders and stones on top the rail section of the bridge."

The levees at Melville and Henderson were breached, flooding everything in the water's path. The attempt at holding down the bridge on the Atchafalaya

Atchafalaya school where Ms. Comeaux taught her students. *Photos courtesy of René Prejean.*

was futile. Part of the bridge collapsed in the river. Delcambre reported that C.R. Shaw said, "The center pier was washed out and leaned downstream, and this pier was 112 feet from top to bottom and it was not possible to salvage." Delcambre said that sometime later, after the water receded, railroad bridge crews "pumped water into a barge to lower it. The barge was then placed in position under the bridge span, and as water was pumped out of the barge, the span was lifted off its piers. The spans were then pulled to the riverbank." Afterward, the bridge spans were floated to the Houston Ship Channel, where they were recycled. The citizens of the Atchafalaya basin prepared "to enter the next decade, but the railroad refused to construct a new bridge," reported Delcambre. By this time, the railroad was still in operation, from Baton Rouge to Atchafalaya and with limited service from Lafayette to Cleon (Henderson).

Moonshining was happening in the basin long before the 1929 depression, and it increased over the years of Prohibition (1920–1933). Delcambre reported that gangsters, such as Al Capone, transported "booze from New Orleans to Chicago and all points between." In 1931, Al Capone used a speedboat that had an auxiliary fuel tank filled with two-hundred-proof moonshine, which probably could have run its engines. That wasn't all; according to Delcambre, basin resident Mulate Guidry stated, "The interior was immaculate, and every door and counter had hidden compartments in which cocaine was found."

It's uncertain who the teachers at Atchafalaya were between 1935 and 1937. Elodie Comeaux of Lafayette taught school there from 1938 to 1940. She walked on the railroad track to meet and ride the U.S. Mail boat to and from school at Atchafalaya. She spent the week at the home of Chunnie and Clarabell Fredrick. On weekends, Comeaux returned to Lafayette. During the 1930s and '40s, she taught school at Central Elementary in Lafayette, where the main library stands today. Other schools were Judice and Golden Meadow. Regardless of where she taught, her sixth-grade classes of mostly twelve-year-olds were required to write essays titled "My Life Story." On August 27, 1951, Ms. Comeaux became Mrs. Prejean when she married J. "Clyde" Prejean and gave up teaching school to raise her family. She and Clyde had four children: René, Celeste, Gordon and David.

Comeaux died in May 2005 at the age of eighty-eight. After her death, family members found a treasure trove of memorabilia in her personal effects. There were nearly one hundred "My Life Story" essays from her former students, all neatly preserved in plastic sheet protectors. Inside each life story folder was each student's black-and-white photo. Some folders contained newspaper clippings of her former students in different periods of their lives: e.g., wedding announcements and anniversaries, personal achievements and a few unfortunate and untimely deaths. Her oldest son, René, began a campaign to find his mother's sixth graders, who by now were grandparents and great-grandparents. René tirelessly searched the internet and telephone directories, seeking by any means necessary to find his mother's former students and return their assignments from sixty years ago. He was highly successful in his endeavors. René said, "It was a humbling experience to see the emotional expression on their faces with tears in their eyes when I gave them their original handwritten essays.

Schoolchildren of Atchafalaya and raised walkways. *Photos courtesy of René Prejean.*

Words could not describe the feelings. It is a sensation I will never forget." It has been said that we will be remembered not by our words but by our kind deeds. Elodie Comeaux Prejean and her son René have certainly displayed kind deeds by their tremendous contribution to preserving the past. I digressed a bit to tell you about Ms. Comeaux and her son René; now, back to Atchafalaya.

Top Row

Floyd   James   Daisy   _Allen   Ezeola _Ethal _ Frank
Devillier Dupuis Zeringue Zeringue Guidry Dupuis Dupuis

Bottom Row

Priscilla Rodney Vivian Leona _Earline _ Alton
Devillier Guidry Montet Devillier Montet   Guidry

Schoolchildren of Atchafalaya school. *Photos courtesy of René Prejean.*

Mulate Guidry was a first-rate fisherman in the Atchafalaya swamp. Delcambre reported that Mulate was the first to catch bass by casting. "From 1952 to 1959, with game warden Gilbert Durand officiating, Guidry caught more than 35,000 bass, not counting the small ones thrown back." By 1951, Mulate Guidry had taken over the dancehall establishment in "New Henderson" and moved it to "its current location in Breaux Bridge."

Southern Pacific Railroad track cart used by Ms. Comeaux to carry her packages and personal belongings to and from the mail boat. *Photo courtesy of René Prejean.*

The coup de grâce for Atchafalaya came after the 1956 flood. That was when the postal service issued its final notice to close the post office at Atchafalaya. In June 1956, the *Postal Service News* vol. 2, no. 6, authored by Marcus M. McWathers, who happened to be the service district superintendent at the time, published an elegant farewell article pertaining to the Atchafalaya basin. The post office door closed for the last time in 1959. Only remnants of the old wooden piles that supported the railroad structure can still be seen, perhaps no more than one hundred yards north of Interstate 10 when traveling west near Pelba. Delcambre reported that what little ground was once claimed as Atchafalaya stands at the Butte La Rose exit along Interstate 10.

Chapter 6

ON VA LES EMBÊTER
(WE WILL TRICK THEM)

One of the most quoted authors regarding Cajun culture is William Faulkner Rushton, a native Louisianian and graduate of USL (UL). His highly acclaimed book *The Cajuns, Acadia to Louisiana* was published in 1979. In Rushton's many chapters regarding Cajuns, one section is devoted to the very first book ever published in Cajun French. That honor goes to Revon Reed from *la grand Louis Durald communauté de Mamou*, in southwest Louisiana. His book was titled *Lache pas la Patate* (*Don't Drop the Potato*), the meaning of which tends to get lost in translation between the two languages. The saying often means "do not drop or lose our Acadian language and heritage." Revon Reed's French reader was published in 1976. My compliments to Richard DesHotels's much appreciated YouTube website that reported Revon Reed was born in 1917 and received a Christian Brothers education. Reed was a World War II longshoreman officer stationed in Okinawa with his *padna* (friend, partner) Pascal Fuselier, both of Mamou. Incidentally, Mamou was established in 1907. After the war and after receiving his master's degree from Boston University, Reed taught school. His teaching career lasted more than thirty-five years.

Besides being an educator, he was also an author, journalist, DJ, publisher and preservationist of the Acadian language and its culture. Reed was also a skillful raconteur. He is probably best remembered as the host of a live radio program in Cajun French every Saturday morning at Alfred "Fred" Tate's Bar in Mamou. The bar is famously known worldwide as Fred's Lounge. Once retired from the school system, Reed wrote his book. It was said to be a vivid description of Louisiana from the perspective of the Acadians. It was a call or reference to our Cajun French language that has been dwindling away for generations, much like Louisiana's coastline. The destruction of Cajun French began in 1921 when French was prohibited on public school grounds—and this was the reason so many young Cajuns wet their pants because they couldn't ask the teacher in English to go to the restroom.

Reed's manuscript, according to Rushton, consisted of not only Cajun French words but also numerous "English words and sounds, and usage— you'll also find miscellaneous scraps from Spanish, German, Portuguese, and Italian, as well as words and ideas taken intact from the cultures of neighboring blacks and Indians." Louisiana and the United States consist of diverse groups of cultures and languages. It would certainly seem appropriate to include those distinctive words from other cultures. America is a melting pot of diverse languages and backgrounds. Not surprisingly, the attitude of the Council for the Development of French in Louisiana (CODOFIL) toward Reed's book was "lukewarm at best," noted Rushton. They mocked Reed's use of words from other cultures. Are the Cajuns the only group to have borrowed words from other ethnicities? I think not.

In July 1968, CODOFIL was "a government funded agency" created with the signing of Louisiana Legislative Act 409. The person who pushed for CODOFIL was none other than James Demengeaux, a Lafayette lawyer and two-term U.S. congressman. Act 409 read, in part, "For the preservation of the *French language as found in Louisiana*" (emphasis mine). However, it was quickly changed to read, "For the development of French in Louisiana." Before the barely noticeable word shift, the legislative enactment meant to protect the Cajun French language that was spoken here for generations. It was the language of our forefathers of Acadie. The Acadians were in North America (old Acadie) since 1604, fifteen years before Christopher Columbus and Plymouth Rock. Our language existed all this time as a spoken language—not a written one. The same is true of our beautiful Cajun music. It was handed down orally. The word *Cajun* is a corruption of the word *Acadian*, much like earlier settlers said "Injun" instead of "Indian." According to Rushton, some linguists say the word *Acadie* is an Indian word for the codfish found in the North Atlantic Ocean. The Acadians were expelled from their homeland in 1755 by *ces maudits Anglais*! Most of the Acadians settled in what was then called the Territory of Louisiana. In 1803, during the signing of the Louisiana Purchase, as a condition of admittance, both the United States and the powers that be over the Territory of Louisiana agreed to accept the population that resided within the area.

Its inhabitants were to be "maintained and protected in the free enjoyment of their liberty, property, and the religion which they profess." Louisiana's first constitution was written in French in 1805, two years after the signing of the Louisiana Purchase. This was well before Louisiana was admitted to the Union in 1812. The state wasn't pressured to write its constitution in English until 1865, after the War Between the States.

Acadiana native Pat Mire's excellent documentary *Mon Cher Camarade*, filmed in 2008, tells an amazing story that had never been told before. Through Mire's camera lens, the story is finally revealed of the hundreds of French-speaking Cajuns who were selected as French interpreters during World War II. In his documentary, mentioned earlier, Dr. Barry Jean Ancelet of UL (now retired) summed it up well when he said, "Isn't it interesting that a language learned with great difficulty from school is considered a mark of culture, but a language learned naturally and spoken fluently from home is considered a problem?" Ancelet went on to say that when CODOFIL was first created in 1968, its name was the Council for the Development of Louisiana French. The name was immediately changed to the Council for French in Louisiana. "There is a big difference," said Ancelet. "My point about this is, if this is just an effort to generate or regenerate generic French; then what is the point? The point should be to preserve the continuity with our own past. If that is the point, we can't regenerate generic French; we have to regenerate this one, with its own particularity and with its own specificity," said Ancelet. *Bien dit*, Barry.

To add insult to injury for the Cajuns, in the 1960s, Hollywood created a television series called *Combat* staring Vic Morrow as Sergeant Chip Saunders and Pierre Jalbert from Quebec, who played PFC Paul "Caje" LeMay, a "real" Cajun GI from New Orleans, of all places! In one scene, Caje was riding a bicycle in the countryside dressed as a civilian Frenchman when he was stopped at a German checkpoint. Caje, the disguised "Cajun GI," was questioned by German soldiers in French, and he was able to answer the questions to their satisfaction. The Germans allowed Caje to continue. I remember viewing that series and silently thinking, He isn't speaking Cajun French. Instead, it was Hollywood's version of what a "real Cajun" should sound like. *Mais, pense donc.* So much for being authentic. In reality, Caje would have been shot because he wasn't speaking the language of the locals in France. He was speaking Canadian French, which is different than Parisian and Cajun French. Apparently, Hollywood thinks all Cajuns live in New Orleans. Pooyie! I digressed a good bit to explain a couple of slights that didn't go unnoticed.

William Rushton argued that the Cajuns borrowed plenty of words from non-French speakers, such as *lagniappe* (a little something extra) from the Spanish word *ñapa*. From the African Americans: *congo* for "water moccasin" and *gris-gris* for "voodoo charm." From the native Americans, we borrowed plenty: e.g., *bayou*, *ouaouaron* for "bullfrog," *plaquemine* for "persimmon," *chaoui* for "raccoon" and *pichouette* for "little girl" or *jeune fille*. From the English we also borrowed an abundance of words, e.g., "peace cop" instead of *agent de police*, "gambler" instead of *gambleur*, "doctor's office" instead of *l'office de docteur* and "movie theater" instead of *la maison de show*, to name a few. In all likelihood, most if not all ethnic words borrowed from the aforementioned cultures would have been irretrievably lost if it were not for some Cajuns determined to keep their language.

Rushton also listed several seventeenth-and-eighteenth-century Acadian words that are nautical in nature and used to describe inland non-nautical words, expressions and areas. For instance, the word *amarrer* means "to moor a boat" and it is also used for knotting one's shoelaces. In standard French, the word would be to *nouer* (tie). Another Cajun French phrase from the maritime Acadians is *virer de bord*, as in "to turn an automobile around" or "to come about, as in a sailboat." In standard French, the word is *tourner*. I would be negligent if I didn't include other nautical or maritime words early Acadians used: e.g., *anse*, for "bay" or "cove," which was used to describe inland non-nautical areas, as in L'anse Grise (Gray Cove), L'anse aux Pailles (Straw Cove) and L'anse Coush-Coush, to name a few. Early Acadians named them "coves" because at the time, the tall grasses swaying in the breeze on the prairies reminded them of waves in a bay or ocean. We also have points, as in the names Pointe Noir (black point), Pointe de Terre (cape or peninsula) and Pointe de Bois (an extended wooded area), used as maritime points of reference for inland non-maritime areas. I'm certain Cajun French words have disappeared because of the English substitution. I strayed a bit to mention borrowed words and phrases. Now, back to Revon Reed, one of the most resilient Acadians in the modern era.

Revon Reed also authored Mamou Prairie, a hometown magazine with a small-town circulation. In Rushton's words, it was "rich in humor, particularly in its tales of *Sosthene* and his dog, *Fideaux*." It was "unlike anything else in English or French journalism." Revon Reed had an amusing explanation of how the name Mamou came about. One version says Mamou is an Indian word from the "Mobilian dialect, an African word for sweetheart, or a word derived from the Russians." He also said a local newspaper once described the area around Mamou as the "mammouth [*sic*] prairie." In keeping with the Cajun tradition of shortening French words, several letters were dropped, which resulted in its current name, Mamou. Reed's tongue-in-cheek version of the name was said to have been conceived when early settlers brought their cattle to the area. "The calves would cry out 'maa' for their dinner; and their mothers would respond with a 'moo.'"

Following is an example of Revon Reed's stories or anecdotes that explained the crucial importance of speaking two languages. First the Cajun French version:

> *Une petite souris était très fière de ses trois petites souris. Un jour elle a décidé d'aller faire une promenade dans la cour. Tout d'un coup un gros chat noir s'est approacher pour les attaquer. Mais le petite mère n'estait pas tracasser du tout. Elle s'est élever sur le bout des ses pattes et elle a commencer a japer comme un gros chien fâché. Le chat, très étonné de ce bruit a foutu le camp bien vite.…Les petites souris étaient bien curieux de tout ça et demande à leur mere pour-quoi le chat s'est sauver aussi vite; et la petite mère a repondu fièrement: "Mais, c'est toujours bon de savoir parler deux langues, mes chers enfants!"*

Following is the English version: A tiny mama mouse took her two little ones for a stroll in the yard. Suddenly, a huge black cat spotted the trio. "What a fine meal," he said to himself. But when he approached the goal, the little mama mouse suddenly turned on the villain and started barking like a fierce dog. The startled cat turned and fled the scene. The little mice couldn't comprehend all this and said so to their mama. "Well," answered mama mouse with pride, "it's still good to speak two languages, my dear children!"

James Donald Faulk authored the first Cajun French grammar book, titled *Cajun French 1*, published in June 1977. Faulk was a former language instructor from Crowley High School. By this time, the government-funded CODOFIL had been established in Louisiana since the summer of 1968 reported Faulk. Instead of teaching Cajun French, which had been spoken in Louisiana since before the United States was formed, the program hired hundreds of foreigners to teach standard French. That probably infuriated Faulk and was the driving force behind his decision to create the Cajun French grammar book. According to Rushton, what annoyed Faulk was when a student complained, "I've been learning French so long, and I still can't speak to my grandma!"

Faulk taught French in Louisiana schools for two decades, wrote Rushton. He was more than aptly qualified to teach French. He "had done undergraduate work in French and Spanish at the University of Southwestern Louisiana [USL, now UL] and graduate work leading to a master's degree from the University of Missouri." It took Faulk three years to complete his 375-page work, which included "an 87-page glossary with more than 3,000 entries." His book sold for $18.95. The first edition of 1,000 copies sold quickly in Louisiana and in other French-speaking areas of the world. Faulk created a phonetic system "based almost entirely on English sounds and wrote all the Cajun French words and phrases in only that phonetic system." This probably made it easier for his students that understood English.

You can imagine CODOFIL's disappointment when Faulk refused to add another column for standard French spellings. *Mais jamais!* Faulk was concerned for the many non-English-speaking Cajuns who lived in rural areas when he wrote "a specialized chapter in Louisiana terms for health and the body." Faulk insisted, "It's for our own good." Faulk wasn't the only one disgruntled with Louisiana's educational system. In 1971, Ed and Catherine Blanchet from the rural community of Meaux in Vermilion Parish were displeased with the school system. To solve the problem, they created their own school and used James Faulk's grammar book. The Blanchet couple taught first through twelfth grade in their four-room schoolhouse, beginning with their seven children. They were more than qualified: Ed and Catherine were trained as schoolteachers. Ed received his training at USL and LSU, while Catherine obtained her education at Sophie Newcomb College and later at USL and LSU.

According to Rushton, at the time of all the hype regarding Cajun French and standard French, Barry Ancelet was director of USL's Cajun folklore center and worked closely with CODOFIL. What Ancelet wanted was for "his students to learn enough 'good' French to be able to communicate with other members of the French community in the world beyond Louisiana, and on an equal basis." Professor Richard Chandler, chairman of foreign languages at USL at the time, suggested that Faulk's course should be taught as an aside course or adjunct from regular classroom studies. I once heard a Cajun French teacher say Cajun French was once offered to students during recess periods. That didn't sit well with the students and teachers.

Rushton reported that once Faulk's grammar book was published in 1977, a group of LSU undergraduates calling themselves Les Cajuns was dead set on forcing LSU to offer a Cajun French course as an elective. That request irritated CODOFIL's chairman, James Demengeaux. The "crusading chairman" of that group was Robert LeBlanc, a geology major from Cameron, Louisiana. Les Cajuns affectionately described

"CODOFIL partisans as *'aristocrottes.'*" Ulysse Richard, a graduate student in linguistics, shed some light on the origin of standard French. Following is Richard's quote: Francien was not adopted as the official language of France until the King's edict of Villers-Cotterêts in 1539, and there were fifteen different dialects from which to choose and standardize a common tongue. However, L'Académie Française—the committee appointed to work out the standardization details—was not organized until 1633, well after immigration to Acadie (1632) had begun. And the Academy's dictionary, which synthesized Burgundian pronunciation and northern grammar, was not issued until 1694. The Cajuns, by then, had their language before there ever was a standard French.

Ulysse Richard admonished anyone who "looks down on the rich Cajun patois and are linguistically naïve." In 1978, Richard authored his own French grammar book, *Lagniappe*: *A Louisiana French Reader*. In 1979, when Rushton's book was published, there was a "resurgence of ethnic pride." Classified newspaper ads were published in all parts of Louisiana for classes in "native French." James Donald Faulk was preparing tapes and workbooks for distribution to "language labs and radio stations," and even "Father Roland Vaugh of *Grand Chênièr*" had prepared a translation of the Mass," reported Rushton. Rushton included an ad from CODOFIL that urged people to speak French: "*Soyez à la mode: parlez française*" (be fashionable: speak French). However, at the time, France's former consul general in New Orleans, Jean-Jacques Peyronner, asked: Which French?

In 1979, there were many who predicted that by the beginning of the twenty-first century, the native French language would have vanished, gone forever. However, according to Rushton, "the Cajuns, resilient as ever, started circulating an underground slogan," which challenged that and other outside assumptions. "*On va les embêter*" was their rallying cry: "We will fool them." By 1978, CODOFIL had a force of forty-three thousand foreign educators in Louisiana funded by state and federal dollars, as well as aid from Canada, France and Belgium, reported Rushton. Try as I might to purchase a copy of James Donald Faulk's book *Cajun French 1*, it was not to be found at any booksellers—although Amazon did report that if they had it, a hardcover copy would cost $265 plus tax and postage. Revon Reed's *Lâche pas la patate: Portrait des Acadiens de la Louisiana* can't be found either. And again, Amazon reported that if they had it, it would cost a whopping $324.99 plus tax and postage for a paperback copy. Thankfully, one of my wife's friends from Abbeville donated a copy of Donald Faulk's *Cajun French 1. Bien merci*, Patty.

Chapter 7

THE POSTAL SERVICE

Sometime back, I interviewed Chester Lee Guidry of Morse, Louisiana. Chester Lee was the postmaster in Morse for more than forty-six years. He informed me that before the town was named Morse in 1900, in honor of Mr. S.F.B. Morse, the general passenger agent for Southern Pacific Railroad, it was named Lorna, which was established in 1898. Back then, Belle Gault was the first postmistress in what was called the "post office store." Belle was the wife of William Gault, who owned the store. Chester Lee Guidry became postmaster of Morse in 1961 when he was every bit of twenty-one years of age. Back then, in order to be hired as either postmaster or rural mail carrier, one had to be approved by the U.S. Congress and served at its discretion. Nelson "Son" Richard of Lyons Point was a Guidry family friend. He informed Chester Lee's father about the opening for the Morse postmaster's job. The job was actually offered to Chester Lee's brother, who at the time had a good-paying job in Lake Charles, so he turned down the offer. Chester Lee was quick to say that he would take it if offered.

Chester, his father and Son Richard went to see Acadia Parish sheriff Elton Arceneaux. It was on a Sunday, recalled Chester Lee. He already had the support of leading citizens: e.g., Jerry Ashley and state legislator Bill Cleveland of Crowley. Sheriff Arceneaux energetically gave his support to Chester Lee for the postmaster position. The sheriff then called his friend, Theo Ashton "T.A." Thomson, state representative of Ville Platte, who was also in favor of Chester Lee. T.A. then called his connection in Washington, D.C., who was Senator Russell B. Long, who also backed Chester Lee for the postmaster position in Morse. Senator Long was able to urge his colleagues in Congress to confirm Chester Lee. A presidential proclamation was signed by President John F. Kennedy confirming Guidry. That is how it was done back then. Chester Lee was confirmed as postmaster for the town of Morse and served at Congress's discretion.

Today, postmasters are promoted from within the postal system. The annual postmaster salary in 1961 was $4,800. In 1961, the Morse post office where Chester Lee was employed was no longer in service. However, it still stands today directly behind Chester Lee's residence in Morse. The old wooden structure was built about 1928 by a Mrs. La Fosse when she became postmistress of Morse, Louisiana. She was followed by Deluke Thibodeaux, who held that position for thirty-three years until he retired in 1961 and was followed by Chester Lee Guidry.

The U.S. postal system dates to colonial days when early Americans wanted to communicate with family members who had stayed behind in England. As the country grew over the years, so did the United States postal service. At one time, it was the United States' greatest undertaking, as chronicled by Winifred Gallagher in his excellent book *How the Post Office Created America*. Unfortunately, the post office was also the United States' least appreciated. At age forty-eight, Benjamin Franklin, one of our founding fathers of the United States, became America's first postmaster. He was the fifteenth child of a candlemaker with barely two years of schooling. Despite his lack of education, he became postmaster and editor-publisher of *Poor Richard's Almanack* and of a prestigious newspaper in the City of Brotherly Love.

Our American mail system was not the first to deliver mail. That distinction belongs to Middle Eastern monarchs four thousand years ago, who used horsemen to deliver messages carved on clay tablets. In addition to the above, the *cursus publicus*—Latin for the "public way," or postal roads—were created expressly for the mounted couriers. The idea of postal roads was about to catch on here when George Washington said, "The importance of the post office and post roads on a plan sufficiently liberal and comprehensive…is increased by their instrumentality in diffusing a knowledge of the laws and proceedings of the government." It became a right of the people to know what was going on in their new republic, or New World, as it was often referred to. Gallagher stated there were 75 post offices and 1,875 miles of post roads in 1790. Mail was notably slow back then—a letter took more than a month to go from Maine to Georgia. George Washington and most politicians back then had envisioned a post office in every town. But the building of post roads was quite different. Gallagher stated that post roads were extremely unpopular back then: "The states regarded the prospect as an invasive threat to their sovereignty."

Benjamin Rush, one of the fifty-six signers of the Declaration of Independence, was a passionate supporter of the mail system and of literacy. Rush's father was a poor dirt farmer who died when Rush was eight years old. No one in his family had ever set foot in a college or university. And as it stood, Rush wasn't going to be the first—at least that is how it appeared. After his father died, Rush's mother sent him to live with an uncle who was a minister and educator so that the boy could have a chance at a proper education. Rush didn't disappoint his mother. He received a medical degree and became a prosperous physician, professor and writer. He knew firsthand the value of an education.

The Post Office Act allowed congressmen and military officers "franking privileges," which allowed them to mail letters or brochures to their constituents and advisors at no cost. When they were left to their own devices, they abused their franking privileges at taxpayer expense. Legislatures overloaded the mail system with long-worded long-winded documents that were referred to as "bunkum," named after Buncombe County, North Carolina. Today, it's often called junk mail. Someone had to pay for the government giveaway. A one-page letter cost between six and twenty-five cents—depending on the distance. Publications such as magazines and pamphlets were charged a slightly higher fee. The Post Office Act created a boom in newspapers across the country. The act mandated that all newspapers were created equal—country publications weren't charged more than urban newspapers.

By 1794, Winifred Gallagher reported, seven-tenths of U.S. mail volume was newspapers, which, to some, helped educate the general public. Benjamin Rush was highly praised for his literacy advocacy. Both Thomas Jefferson and John Adams delivered his eulogy. Rush had long advocated for newspaper circulation and the information the newspapers contained. Contrary to the beliefs of Benjamin Rush and many other early Americans, England initially disallowed the publication of newspapers, believing they would provoke a rebellion. America's Post Office Act included a law that banned the opening of letters or packages by anyone other than the addressee. Back then, people often sent money through the mail. The act also made it a crime to steal mail, punishable by death. However, by 1799, the law was amended: the first offense was forty lashes and jail time. Additionally, the U.S. mail took precedence: "All teams and vehicles were prompt to give way." The "mail must not be obstructed or delayed for a moment." Living near a "major postal route" greatly increased property value.

Steamboats significantly improved the mail system thanks to Robert Fulton's invention of the steam engine in 1807. Remember writing "airmail" on letters before nearly all mail was sent by air? Well, back in the early 1800s, "steam" or "steamboat" was written on letters. By 1810, there were 2,300 post offices and 36,000 miles of post roads. As indicated by Gallagher, twenty years later, that number had nearly quadrupled. In 1815, a two-page letter sent from Ohio to Virginia cost fifty cents. About 1831, railroads began to be built in America. A year later, in 1832, under President Andrew Jackson's administration, the mail was authorized to travel by train. Jackson was an advocate for the post and its expansion. At that time, America had "twice as many post offices as Great Britain and five times more than France." Early postal workers "walked an average of twenty miles per day, fifty-two weeks per year until the 1880s." At that time, they began to receive two weeks' vacation and worked an eight-hour day. And back then, citizens were not required to have mailboxes because the mailman had to personally hand-deliver the mail to their customers. If the homeowner was not home, the mailman would attempt to deliver the mail on his next trip. And as the author indicated, most letter carriers had wooden knockers to protect their knuckles. By 1923, homeowners were required to have mailboxes.

Old Hickory, as President Andrew Jackson was often referred to, was an outsider in Washington, D.C. Gallagher reported that Jackson wanted to transform Washington. He wanted to decrease the size of government and rid Washington of corruption and the age-old practice of awarding federal jobs to Washington insiders—thus inspiring a new adage along the way, by New York senator William L. Marcy, who said, "To the victor belongs the spoils." According to the author, Jackson fired about "13% of federal workers despite merit." They were "National Republicans." Jackson awarded those jobs to average citizens who became his base. He created a "rotation of office" policy, wrote Gallagher. From every region of the of the country, Jackson's constituents loved him. Conversely, "his opponents hated him and referred to the president as Andrew Jackass," which is how the donkey or jackass became the Democrat's symbol.

As we know, elections do have consequences. The process of firing the opposition's staff or party members after each newly elected president continued for nearly 150 years. And as Chester Lee Guidry, the longtime resident and former postmaster of Morse, can attest, he was the last postmaster to have gone through the process of being confirmed by Congress in 1961.

SPECIAL THANKS TO WINIFRED Gallagher for his excellent book *How the Post Office Created America*, *et a gros bien merci pour* Chester Lee Guidry and Jerry Clark of Morse for their assistance with this story.

Chapter 8

THE PLAQUEMINE POINT SHOOTOUT

This story is about a gun battle that occurred at Plaquemine Point, Louisiana, in 1924. According to an article in the *Port Arthur News*, one of the fiercest gun battles ever fought in St. Landry Parish occurred six miles southwest of Lawtell at Joseph Dejean's Garage. The garage doubled as the voting precinct for Plaquemine Point. The incident came to be known as the "election day shootout," which resulted in the deaths of three well-known citizens of the Sixth Ward of St. Landry Parish and the wounding of four others. The gunfight was the culmination of ill feelings of eight years earlier.

A few weeks before the September 9, 1924 election, Joseph Cormier and several members of John Childs's clan just happened to be at a nearby cotton gin in Lewisburg, Louisiana. Both factions met at the cotton gin, which may have been planned or prearranged. Member of John Childs's family allegedly attacked Joseph Cormier with knives, slashing him severely. Cormier was sent to the Opelousas sanitarium, where some thought he would die. A few days before the election of 1924, Cormier discharged himself from the sanitarium.

Before we get into the meat of the story, let us see what else was taking place in 1924: Prohibition was alive and well. Calvin Coolidge (R) was president, the first president to use radio. The governor of Louisiana was Henry Luse Fuqua Sr. (D). He had defeated Huey Long and two others in an earlier election. Fuqua died halfway into his term. Henry Ford was still building Model T automobiles (since 1908) in any color, as long as it was black. The Model A was not built until 1928. This was the year that Euzebe Vidrine, the serial killer, paid for his crimes. The following were born in 1924: Jimmy Carter, Lee Iacocca, Doris Day and Marlon Brando. And so was my father, the late Wilson Thibodeaux, on October 26, 1924.

Now, returning to the shootout at Plaquemine Point. Joseph Cormier allegedly sent word to the Childs family members saying he would get them yet. Another newspaper article reported that at the time of the knifing, Joseph Cormier said, "Tom Childs, I'll get you yet." No one is certain of how many Childs family members took part during the slashing of Cormier. However, what led to the altercation supposedly happened eight years earlier, when Thomas Childs was thirteen years of age. This is what allegedly happened when young Thomas Childs kept throwing dirt clods or rocks at parish road crews when they were either constructing or widening a road across from the Childs place. Joseph Cormier was an election official for Plaquemine Point; at least one newspaper mistakenly referred to it as Plaquemine Ridge. Regardless, it happened at Joseph Dejean's Garage at Plaquemine Point, which is at the edge of the St. Landry Parish line across from the Acadia Parish community of Pitreville. Pitreville is located along what is now Highway 358, which runs in an east–west direction, and Pitreville is just west of Highway 35, which runs in a north–south direction from Lawtell to Church Point and Rayne. Plaquemine Point is a stone's throw from that 90-degree turn between Highway 358 and Highway 35. Both are in St. Landry Parish's Sixth Ward.

Joseph Nathan Cormier was inside the garage (voting precinct) when John Childs and his son, Thomas, ambled into the polling place. According to an Associated Press newspaper article datelined from Opelousas, John Childs started the gunfight by firing first, although other news publications reported that Cormier fired first. After Childs fired his handgun, Cormier quickly pulled his revolver and fired, immediately dropping the elder Childs. Thomas Childs reached for his gun, but he was too slow. Thomas Childs was dead before he hit the floor. Getty Childs, another son of John Childs, probably entered the garage a few seconds behind the others and also got into the fray. During the free-for-all shootout, the Associated Press reported, Joseph Cormier was shot six times and, while lying on the floor, managed to calmly reload his gun and continued shooting his assailant before dying within minutes. Getty Childs was so badly injured no one expected him to live.

Brothers Arville and Jean Baptiste Richard along with Joseph Castille were there to help either Cormier or the Childs family. However, they were perhaps just innocent bystanders who were wounded during the scuffle. Regardless, Elton "Bee" Cormier said Arville was shot in the face by a glancing bullet, while Jean Baptiste was shot in the back and Castille received a bullet to the abdomen. Despite all being seriously wounded, the three men were said to have survived the shooting spree. According to Al Bethard (now deceased), formerly employed by UL University's Dupré Library, the Childs family migrated to the area from Arkansas shortly after the War Between the States. The Associated Press reported that "Joseph Cormier was one of the largest landowners in St. Landry Parish."

Over the years, there were several family members named Nathan Cormier. I spoke to one of the relatives with that name about the shootout perhaps a decade or more ago. He said that he was told the story many years earlier when he was a young boy attending St. Francis Catholic School of Iota. One afternoon, he missed the bus and was forced to walk home. As he walked, a stranger in an automobile stopped and asked if he wanted a ride. Nathan said he didn't know the man but got into the car anyway. The driver was making small talk and asked, "What's your name?" The young boy replied, "Nathan Cormier." The stranger driving the automobile immediately locked his brakes as the vehicle skewed and slid forward on the loose gravel. The expression on the stranger's face instantly changed from courteous to an almost unrecognizable look of what appeared to be excruciating pain as he shouted, "Get out of the car, now!"

When Nathan finally made it home, his father, Evans Cormier, asked what happened. Nathan explained the story about missing the bus and the weird encounter with the stranger. Nathan's father told him about the shootout and the long-running family feud between the Cormier and Childs families. According to Nathan, the stranger in the automobile was Getty Childs; against all odds, he did survive his near-fatal ordeal. His serious wounds left him badly crippled. He later became a traveling salesman peddling Watkins home products from the trunk of his car. It was said that when Getty Childs made his calls, he always offered Lifesaver candies to the children. He was best remembered by many as the Watkins man.

Back to the shooting. Both families, the Childs and Cormier family, were said to stand high in the community and have many friends. The sheriff and coroner of Opelousas were sent to the scene of the tragedy. I spoke about the shootout on election day in 1924 with Elton Cormier, who said what led to the incident at Plaquemine Point had something to do with Spanish land grants of old. When the land grants were issued, there were no provisions for rights of way or easements for roadways. It was open range; you could travel in any direction, or you could follow what were then called Indian trails. The task of land grant easements and building roads later became the responsibility of St. Landry Parish and was implemented by the police jury system. Joseph Cormier was an employee of the St. Landry Parish Police Jury, and he was assigned the task of overseeing the building and maintaining of roads throughout the parish. When parish employees were building a road that bordered the Childs property, a young boy—a member of the Childs family—probably Thomas Childs—threw dirt clods at the parish employees, which prevented them from performing their assignments.

Joseph Cormier was notified to talk to the youngster. Cormier advised the boy this was now public property and to discontinue his rude behavior. The boy continued and, again, Cormier was notified. Again, he had a discussion with the youngster; however, this time Joseph Cormier informed the ill-mannered youngster that if he persisted, he would personally plant his foot up the boy's derriere. As the story goes, Cormier followed through with his promise. The boy ran home and complained to his father, John Childs. Years later, several Childs family members caught up with Joseph Cormier, and a knife-wielding battle ensued, with Joseph receiving the brunt of the injuries. Joseph Cormier landed in the Opelousas sanitarium for three weeks and was strongly advised not to return to work.

It was rumored that Cormier had sent word to the Childs family that he would seek revenge and they would pay with their lives. On the morning of election day, September 9, 1924, Joseph Cormier assembled a few well-armed friends to accompany him. Cormier allegedly instructed the men not to fire before he fired. It was also alleged that John Childs had a few friends with guns to accompany the Childs clan. All thoughts of fighting vanished when Childs's friends arrived at Dejean's garage. It was alleged that after the shooting, the pungent smell of blood mixed with cordite hung in the air like a thick fog. The inside of Dejean's garage was littered with bullet holes—bright shafts of sunlight like an Edward Hopper painting could be seen coming through the thin walls.

Many years ago, Elton "Bee" Cormier was employed by Theo Daigle and Brothers of Church Point. He was informed by the office manager to never reveal his last name to Darrell Childs. Bee was curious and wanted to know why. The office manager proceeded to tell the story of the family feud and the subsequent shootout at Joseph Dejean's Garage. Bee knew all about the incident at the polling place and could have given the office manager much more information. A few weeks later, Darrell Childs walked into Theo Daigle's store, and Bee waited on the man. The two got along well, and when their business was over, Darrell introduced himself as Darrell Childs and asked, "What's your name?" Elton said, "It's Elton Cormier, but everyone calls me Bee." Without saying a word, Darrell Childs immediately spun on his heels and exited the store without his items.

Elton knew without a doubt the old family feud was alive and well. He walked to the manager's office and informed his supervisor what had just transpired. The manager said, "Looks like we just lost a good customer." Nearly two weeks later, in walked Darrell Childs. Bee noticed when he walked in and told one of the other clerks to assist him, but the old gentleman declined. He specifically asked for Bee Cormier. Darrell Childs walked up to Bee with a pleasant smile on his face as he extended his right hand to shake Bee's hand. Bee said he was afraid because he knew of people who were offered a hand to shake while the other held a knife. Bee readily accepted his hearty handshake, as he could see sincerity in the man's eyes. Darrell Childs said, "You and I had nothing to do with what happened to our families years ago. I think you're a very nice young man. Please accept my apology." Bee thanked the man and accepted his apology. From that point on, each time the old gentleman came into the hardware store, he would seek out Bee Cormier to assist him. Bee said he kept waiting and hoping that one day Darrell Childs would talk about the incident at Plaquemine Point, but he never did. Bee said it was the beginning of a long friendship.

Elton "Bee" Cormier of Church Point was inducted into the Cajun Music Hall of Fame in 1997. In 2012, he was inducted into the Living Legends program of the Acadian Museum in Erath. Bee Cormier died in 2018 at the age of eighty-four.

Chapter 9

THE MIDLAND BRANCH RAILROAD AS SEEN THROUGH NEWSPAPER ARTICLES

The Midland Branch railroad line was built in five segments. The first section was the salt mine railroad. This rail line went from New Iberia to Avery Island, about a 5-mile distance. The rail line was named the I&V (Iberia & Vermilion) railroad. At I&V junction, there was a track diversion where the Midland railroad branch began, 5.4 miles west of New Iberia. In other words, the salt mine railroad continued straight toward Avery Island, while the Midland Branch had a slight dogleg right. From that turnout or railroad switch, the Midland Branch continued in a westerly direction. Once all five sections—mile post 0 to mile post 89 (New Iberia to Mamou)—were completed, it was then called the Midland Branch. However, not to be confused, I must mention that New Iberia is a railroad station on the former Southern Pacific's main track (mile post 125.6) between New Orleans and Lafayette, Louisiana, as it is still today.

The Midland Branch went westward once it left New Iberia, and the line went through several railroad stations, including Rynella, Lee Station, Poufette, Bob Acres and Meadows, before arriving at Delcambre, Erath, Abbeville, Kaplan, Mulvey and then Gueydan. At Gueydan, the line turned northward and went through the stations of Riceville, Morse and Midland (mile post 56.3), which was also on Southern Pacific's main track (mile post 181.9) approximately halfway between New Orleans and Houston. Trains continuing northward on the Midland Branch toward Eunice had to cross Southern Pacific's main track at Midland via a wye track. Once back on the branch line, it was thirty-three miles to Mamou (mile post 89), where, at one time, the railroad interchanged with the CRI&P (Chicago, Rock Island and Pacific Railroad). The branch line between Mamou and Eunice, which was nine and a half miles, was abandoned and taken up sometime before 1935. The rest of the rail line (Eunice to New Iberia) was eventually sold in the 1980s (slightly more than one hundred years since the railroad's arrival in March 1880 at Vermilionville). The rail line was sold to the L&D (Louisiana and Delta Railroad), a short line railroad, part of the Genesee & Wyoming property. Most of the railroad between Eunice and Abbeville was taken up sometime in the 1980s.

Before the Midland Branch was constructed, the local citizenry had to wait for the railroad construction crews to complete the main track, main track sidings and higher priority branch lines. The populace was frustrated; they wanted a railroad and they wanted to know when they were going to get it. The following is a chronological list of events documented in actual newspaper articles that show early railroad-related developments of Southern Pacific's Midland Branch in southwest Louisiana:

September 17, 1881
The *Meridional* newspaper of Abbeville asked, "What has become of the railroad from here [Abbeville] to New Iberia?" So far, it was all talk, and the people were frustrated. They wanted to see action! Everyone knew a rail line was needed and it would soon pay for itself in little or no time. But when? That was the $64,000 question everyone was asking. The first segment of the railroad was built in 1883 between New Iberia and Avery Island. Next, the railroad between Abbeville and I&V Junction was completed in 1892. The third section of the railroad construction began from Midland to Gueydan and was completed in 1898. The portion of railroad between Eunice to Mamou was completed about 1900. Mamou was where the railroad interchanged freight railcars with the outside world through the Rock Island railroad. The final segment of railroad between Gueydan and Abbeville began in June 1901 and was completed eleven months later in May 1902. Following are newspaper articles before the arrival of the railroad.

March 24, 1883
The *Meridional* newspaper reported its editor was happy to learn that the citizens of New Iberia were keeping up the movement for a railroad from the salt mine to Abbeville. And they hoped that by the end of 1883, the railroad would be completed. They weren't giving up until they were victorious.

April 28, 1883

The headline of the *Meridional* read: "Important Notices." The paper was happy to report that the New Iberia and Salt Mine Railroad was pushing on toward Abbeville. All that stood in the way was the approval of the right-of-way from the landowners. A survey of the area was scheduled to take place in the not-too-distant future.

May 26, 1883

The *Meridional* reported that the rail line named the New Iberia and Salt Mine Railroad would be in running order by June. A committee from New Iberia were scheduled to visit Abbeville the following week to prepare for a rail line between the two municipalities.

June 16, 1883

The citizenry of Abbeville was also thinking about a possible rail line from their city to Broussardville or Lafayette, which might be more enticing than going to New Iberia. Afterall, Lafayette was becoming a railroad hub. Their mindset was that after its completion, the yet-to-be-built "Vermilionville and Port Allen railroad" would be a more direct route to get their products to market. The newspaper editor added that it was not his domain to decide such things. You can almost feel the frustration from these newspaper articles regarding the slow coming of the railroad, which did not arrive in Abbeville until nearly ten frustrating years later.

In 1890, in the vicinity of where the town of Gueydan would eventually be established, Jean Pierre Gueydan, a native of France, began preparing for a town and an eventual railroad. Gueydan came to Louisiana as a young man sometime before the War Between the States. After much traveling for several years in Louisiana and Texas, he purchased nineteen thousand acres of mostly marshland in western Vermilion Parish for twelve and a half cents an acre. He later completely encircled all his property by fence—the entire eleven-mile-long-by-six-mile-wide property. At that time, Gueydan's property was referred to as the Gueydan Pasture.

January 25, 1890

A public announcement was published in the *Meridional*, notifying the public of an agricultural company being formed to cultivate rice on lands rented from J.P. Gueydan. The article then advised "To Whom It May Concern" that Gueydan's pasture would be closed and completely encircled by fence beginning on the first of January 1890. The article went on to advise whoever had cattle grazing within the enclosure that they were now required to remove their livestock immediately. Along with that, the article also advised that hunting on said property was no longer allowed. It closed by stating, "Anyone found hunting within the Gueydan enclosure, rented by the undersigned, shall be strictly dealt with according to law." Following are the names of the undersigners: Charles Hungerford, George Hanffman, Thomas Inman, James H. Smith, Ernest Montagne, A.J. Lepretre, Henry Swit, Remy Boyer, Paul Trahan, Adam Istre, Andre Suir Jr., Etienne Benoit, Edmond Creider, Alfred Benoit, J.N. Shoemaker, J.H. Dawson, Flacide Mouton, Harry Merriman, Sylvaneus Gotreaud, Henry Flory, Numah LeBlanc, Guy DeBlanc, Paul Montague and Polive Manceau.

September 19, 1891

A conference was held in Abbeville by some the leading citizens the previous week. Preliminary steps were taken to drum up support for a five-mill tax, levied for ten years, to be used to entice the SPRR (Southern Pacific Railroad) to create a rail line to Abbeville. The tax was also to be used for the right-of-way and to secure property for a depot. The *Lafayette Advertiser* newspaper mentioned that New Iberia had already voted on a similar tax tendered to Southern Pacific for a rail line.

November 17, 1891

A headline in the *Meridional* read, "Railroad Meeting: Abbeville, La." Many citizens of Abbeville and Vermilion Parish, including most of the railroad executive committee, met at the courthouse on November 6, 1891. The committee chose J.H. Putnam as its chairman and Dr. C.J. Edwards as secretary. The minutes were read and adopted. At this meeting, letters from J. Kruttschnitt, the general manager of SPRR, were read, stating that Southern Pacific Railroad would construct a railroad to Abbeville provided the town of Abbeville supplied a five-mill tax for ten years. Southern Pacific Railroad also wanted the town to furnish a depot site and right-of-way for the railroad free of charge. The consensus of the members was that the railroad's proposal was doable. A motion was made to appoint a committee to see if the townspeople would agree to such a tax if put to a vote. Another committee of three was appointed to "secure by donation the necessary depot grounds in Abbeville in immediate vicinity thereof and the right-of-way through the parish."

Julius Kruttschnitt was a native of New Orleans and apparently was well liked by all who knew him. Kruttschnitt followed in the footsteps of Collis Potter Huntington and Edward Henry Harriman, early icons of the rail industry. Unfortunately, Kruttschnitt died only days after his retirement on May 31, 1925. The town of Morse, Louisiana, named an avenue in his honor. *Author's collection.*

February 20, 1892

The *Meridional* reported that on Tuesday, E.B. Cushing, the person in charge of the engineering corps surveying the proposed railroad right-of-way on what was then referred to as the Salt Mine branch to Abbeville, had reached town. The party inspected the areas it was instructed to. That evening, General Manager J. Kruttschnitt inspected the three site offers. Kruttschnitt was most impressed with the site "just below town on the Godchaux place." It was also reported that the site chosen by the railroad general manager could not be obtained by law. It would take time and money before a depot site was decided. The first train entered Gueydan in 1889. The townspeople came out to see history in the making. The extension (Midland to Gueydan) cost Southern Pacific $75,000.

October 8, 1892

The *Lake Arthur Herald* reported that the Duson Bros. of Crowley had purchased thirteen thousand acres of land from J.P. Gueydan, inside the pasture, and expected to build a town. The Duson brothers built several

Left: Walter Webb "W.W." Duson, newspaper owner/editor, also an early real estate developer who built several towns on the windswept prairies of Vermilion, Evangeline and Acadia Parishes. Photo circa 1905. *Courtesy of Freeland Archives and Acadia Parish Library in Crowley, Louisiana.*

Right: Cornelius Curly "C.C." Duson, former sheriff of St. Landry Parish, U.S. marshal and real estate developer. *Courtesy of Freeland Archives and Acadia Parish Library in Crowley, Louisiana.*

towns in southwest Louisiana, including Riceville, Morse, Midland, Crowley, Duson, Eunice and Mamou. The well-known brothers and Southern Pacific Railroad were instrumental in populating southwest Louisiana. They are also credited with bringing hardworking wheat farmers and their families from Union and Parke Counties in western Indiana to settle on the prairies of southwest Louisiana. These farmers became some of the best rice growers in the country.

November 26, 1892

The *Crowley Signal* newspaper reported that "Col. Garland and son, of Parke County, Indiana, arrived here last Wednesday with two carloads of mules and farming implements." The equipment was said to be worth about $3,000, and the Garlands were storing it on the farm of S.E. Linebarger until they could erect buildings on the section of land they purchased in the Gueydan pasture. The article concluded with welcoming Mr. Garland and his son to southwest Louisiana. The railroads of southwest Louisiana were still in their early stages, and everyone wanted a railroad to their part of the world. Back then, cities either prospered or died on the vine depending on if they had a rail line or not. As you will see in the following pages, city leaders did all they could to obtain the services of a rail line.

December 10, 1892

"Our friends on Lake Arthur are now looking for the railroad as eagerly as we once did." It is evident from this statement that everyone, every municipality in the state, wanted a rail line in their hometown. Back then, Lake Arthur was known as the Garden Spot of the South. Lake Arthur boasted about being an earthly paradise and having a sufficient population for their Shangri La with a good church and school. At the time when this statement was published, there were bids for the construction of a high school building. The townsfolk were hoping to get a rail line from Abbeville, but as fate would have it, their railroad came from Lake Charles. Oftentimes, in the 1980s and 1990s, railroaders in the engineering and operating department of the Southern Pacific Railroad discussed and asked why the railroad had not constructed a rail line to bridge the gap between Gueydan and Lake Arthur. It would have certainly benefited the railroad and its customers in the event of a major train derailment or other disasters on Southern Pacific Railroad's main track. An interesting article from the *Jennings Daily Record* of January 17, 1902, mentioned building a railroad toward Lake Arthur—however, "through the Lacassine country to Lakeside." Lakeside is situated on the south side of the lake. If the rail line had been built to Lakeside, there probably would not be Lake Arthur. The community of Lakeside had visions of being a major resort. Unfortunately, two successive hard freezes not only destroyed the fruit and vegetables but also ruined the chances of a Lakeside resort. Oh, what could have been.

December 15, 1892

Headline: "The Celebration." Thursday, December 15, 1892, was a day that was probably remembered for a long time in Abbeville. That was the day the train tracks made it to Abbeville. A committee of three, Drs. W.D. White, W.G. Kibbe and J.H. Putnam, decorated the front entrance of "the new depot with cane, cotton, and rice, in their natural state, and festoons of Spanish moss." The people were pleased at how quickly the railroad dream had turned into a reality. What a great Christmas gift to the citizens of Abbeville after waiting since 1880 for a railroad.

Crowley, Acadia Parish seat, established 1887. *Photo courtesy of Freeland Archive and Acadia Parish Library in Crowley, Louisiana.*

The stores and business places of Abbeville had closed at two thirty, and a large portion of the population of the town gathered at the new train depot to welcome the special train containing the Southern Pacific Railroad officials as well as the city fathers of New Iberia and its newspapermen. Historically, on Southern Pacific Railroad, all extra trains such as this one were called specials, which dates to the beginning of railroading. At one period, probably in the 1920s, trains had names, not numbers—names are more romantic than numbers. Some of the names of passenger trains were the Hummingbird, the Blue Bird, the Bon-Air Special and the granddaddy of them all, the Sunset Limited, which is the oldest passenger train in the United States, since 1894—and it still operates right through the heart of Acadiana.

The SPRR officers' special was due in Abbeville at three o'clock, but—as happens in many cases, especially on such occasions—the train was not on time. The train finally arrived at four forty-five. The special was composed of two sleepers, Guadeloupe and Morgan, and one coach. The reception committee detrained and was escorted to the depot platform. The committee members were Messrs. Julius Kruttschnitt, general manager of Southern Pacific Railroad; the president of the I&VRR; J.G. Schreiver, Southern Pacific Railroad traffic manager; Wm. F. Owens, Southern Pacific Railroad superintendent; E.B. Cushing, Southern Pacific Railroad chief engineer; A.

Vermilion Parish Courthouse (third structure built), the last constructed in 1953 in the beautiful downtown square with its massive live oaks in the heart of Abbeville, Louisiana. *Author's collection.*

C. Pickett, vice president of the I&VRR; Mayor Koch of New Iberia; and several other prominent dignitaries.

According to the *Meridional*, Kruttschnitt was formally presented to J.H. Putnam, chairman of the Citizens Railroad committee. Putnam made an elaborate address to welcome everyone, which was responded to in a few appropriate remarks by Kruttschnitt, who called on Robert F. Broussard of New Iberia (who later became a U.S. representative and a U.S. senator from Louisiana) to speak on behalf of the railroad. Afterward, there were salvos of artillery and screeching of whistles. After Kruttschnitt's remarks, the group was taken to the masonic hall, where a banquet was held for the visitors. Toasts were proposed by "Judge Allen, Judge Debaillon, Messrs. Putnam, W.A. White, Mayor Koch, Millard, and a number of other gentlemen."

December 17, 1892
Headline: "The First Train." "The long looked for, wished for and yes even prayed for event has transpired." Abbeville at long last had its railroad. On Thursday, December 15, 1892, at 8:30 a.m., the first train departed from the depot at Abbeville on schedule. It was made up of a combination of car no. 457 and passenger coach 408, drawn by engine 512 with Joe Hannon in the locomotive cab and Conductor Marye in charge of his train. The train

was to be at its terminal in New Iberia at 10:40 a.m., making the run in 2 hours and 10 minutes. At the time, the stations from Abbeville going toward New Iberia were Erath, Meadows, Bob Acres, Poufette, Lee and Salt Mine Junction. The total distance is 21½ miles, and the fare cost 85 cents each way. Returning trains would leave New Iberia at 3:00 p.m. and arriving at Abbeville at 5:10 p.m. Oh how I remember those stations well. I rode the rails on the Midland Branch in the 1970s and again in the early 1990s and can attest that the aforementioned stations were still in SPRR's timetable, with the addition of Delcamre and Rynella and the exclusion of Meadows, which was replaced with Gross Isle.

January 14, 1893

The headline in the *New Delta* of New Iberia read, "Louisiana Is the Place." The article reported the following:

> *To those in search of homes, Louisiana can justly lay claim to more natural advantages than any state in the union. Among those advantages may be enumerated climate, soil inexhaustible waterways, as well as railroad facilities to meet the wants of shippers in parishes remote from main lines, and last but not least a state equal to any in point of health. Ye denizens of the North, East and West, think of a favored locality on this continent where flowers bloom in the open air the year round, where in midwinter the icy finger of King Frost is seldom laid on the most delicate plant.*

Ads such as this were commonplace in the late 1800s. Southern Pacific Railroad and the Duson brothers from Crowley used some of the same verbiage to entice buyers.

The article continued by stating how great Vermilion Parish was. It reported how mild its winters were. They were so mild that very little fuel was required to adequately heat homes, compared to northern states. It also boasted about tenant farming, about how one sharecropper in the parish of Vermilion was without a dollar and had everything furnished; he was paid $1,500. After paying living expenses for the year, which included rent, use of mule or horse team, feed and other expenses, totaling $750, the sharecropper made $750. The article continued once more about the weather. It stated that Vermilion's climate was so mild that "farming is scarcely interrupted for a week in twelve months of the year. It could be considered an advantage over any portion of the West, where farming is limited to six months and where a large percentage of their products are necessary to winter stock."

If You Lived In
WRIGHT
You'd Be Home Now

Wright rice dryer. The sign made countless individuals reflect deeply on their life choices. I was certainly taken aback the first time I saw it while riding the rails on a cold winter's day in the early 1970s. *Author's collection.*

We certainly do not want to leave out the beautiful *Alice LeBlanc*, a passenger steamer owned by J.H. Putnam and Eli Wise. The steamboat would run "in connection with the Southern Pacific Road, carrying freight and passengers both above and below Abbeville." The *New Delta* listed its hands, of which the officers were "George George master; G. Godchaux clerk; Jas N. Roberts pilot; Steward Miller mate; Frank De Heaven first engineer; and Richard Woods second engineer." The article reported on the grand view from the deck of the *Alice LeBlanc*. "One gets a view, which for picturesque beauty is hardly equaled anywhere in the South. Reflecting the soft rays of a tropical sun, the waters of the Vermilion, like a silver thread follows its winding channel through the lowlands to be met in time by the restless waves of the great ocean."

July 22, 1893

The railroad team included General Manager Julius Kruttschnitt, Superintendent W. F. Owens, Judge J.G. Parkerson and Randolph Natili of Southern Pacific Railroad. They were talking with a group of businessmen from the Breaux Bridge area about the "possibility and feasibleness" of constructing a branch rail line from Lafayette to Breaux Bridge and Arnaudville. Kruttschnitt stated how impressed he was with "the eagerness and plausibility of the representatives" of the area, who were "Drs. H.P. Guilbeau and F.R. Martin, and Messrs. A.F. Domengeaux, Chas Babin, and L.C. Guidry of Breaux Bridge, and a Lafayette group, e.g., Messrs. Crow Girard, H.A. Vander Cruyssen, Julian Mouton and Dr. N.P. Moss." Kruttschnitt informed the committee that "in the event of the branch road being built, no actual work in that direction could take place this year." The meeting ended on good terms without making any promises. Everyone wanted a rail line, but it was slow at coming. During that era, the railroads in south Louisiana were still in their formative years. Despite the panic of 1893, railroads were being built in nearly every part of the state, and everyone feared being left behind.

October 14, 1893

"We have heard the railroad is coming through sure, but we have heard that for two years. Every Fall the railroad breeze blows, and few fellows buy land on the strength of good talk; and still, we are 20 miles away from market."

According to the *Gueydan Journal* of November 20, 1900, "Mr. Pierre Gueydan began offering incentives to Southern Pacific Railroad to construct an eleven-

The Gueydan Museum and Cultural Arts Society of Gueydan, Louisiana. The impressive structure was originally the Bank of Gueydan, built in 1902—the first bank to serve the community of Gueydan. *Author's collection.*

The beautiful wooden sculpture of Mr. Jean Pierre Gueydan, founder of Gueydan, is on display at the Gueydan Museum and Cultural Arts Society. The extraordinary carving was sculpted and donated by Joseph Boatner Hebert. *Author's collection.*

mile branch line from Midland to the new town he began as the Town of Gueydan. Gueydan deeded a whole section of land [one square mile or 640 acres] to the railroad as a right-of-way through his land and new town tract."

April 6, 1895
"E.A. Dampier and Robert Wimberley will open a store in the Gueydan neighborhood near the head of the Gueydan Canal. The building having already been completed." —*Crowley Signal*

April 27, 1895
"J.N. Fonts, of the Garland Ranch was in town Sunday and he informs us that the Gueydan irrigating canal is nearly completed, and that they would begin pumping this week in order to test the permeability of the levees, when the water is against them." —*Abbeville Meridional.* Years ago, numerous man-made canals carried water for countless miles over the prairies of southwest Louisiana for rice irrigation. The canals were powered by massive steam turbines, which pumped water from the many bayous and waterways. Some of these canals were two hundred feet wide by six feet deep, and the levees were usually inspected twice daily on horseback looking for damaged levees or for signs of individuals illegally taking water. Lawsuits were sometimes brought against people for nonpayment. The cost for obtaining water for rice irrigation was usually one-fifth of the rice harvest. The use of irrigation canals was discontinued and they were drained and filled in sometime in the 1970s, when rice farmers had their own electric deepwater wells or the use of mechanical PTOs (power take-offs).

May 25, 1895
"The Southern Pacific engineers a few days ago completed the survey of the Southern Extension of the Midland Branch, which will be about twelve miles in length. Grading will commence within a month." —The *Meridional.* The branch rail line between Midland and Gueydan was known as the Southern Extension.

August 3, 1895
"In anticipation of the early completion of the southern extension on the Midland Branch a new town has been laid off on the west side of the survey on the lands of Susie and Alcee Broussard, which we understand is to be called Riceville." —*Crowley Signal.* The town of Riceville is situated on the northern edge of Vermilion Parish. The town site consisted of fifty-three

lots. They were 66 by 182 feet. It was reported that the grading work on the Southern Extension was nearly complete. Riceville is the first community south of Bayou Queue de Tortue (Turtle Tail Bayou), which is the boundary separating Vermilion and Acadia Parish.

August 10, 1895

The *Crowley Signal* reported that the new town on the prairie named Gueydan was making "preliminary arrangements for the grading of streets and for the construction of sidewalks, and for the planting of shade trees." The Duson brothers were the ones grading streets and planting shade trees.

August 25, 1895

The *Meridional* reported that the construction material for a new hotel was now on the ground, waiting to be used. No name was given for the new hotel.

October 26, 1895

The *New Orleans Picayune* was proud to report that the railroad from Midland to Gueydan would be completed in about three weeks' time. It stated, "The pile driver would begin work on Wednesday or Thursday over Bayou *Queue de Tortue.*" It concluded by reporting that the "bridge master" from the Louisiana Western Division oversaw construction of the bridge. The town of Morse was a railroad station between Riceville and Midland. A narrow avenue parallels the old roadbed where the Midland branch line once existed. A street there still bears the name "Kruttschnitt," as in Julius Kruttschnitt (1854–1925), a well-respected former chairman of Southern Pacific Railroad and native of New Orleans. According to a well-written book titled *The Southern Pacific 1901–1985* by Don L. Hofsommer, Kruttschnitt was known in railroad circles as the Von Moltke of transportation. He was born in New Orleans and graduated from Washington and Lee University with a degree in civil engineering. He taught for five years and then realized his boyhood dream of becoming a railroader. Kruttschnitt began his railroad career in Louisiana in 1878 with Charles Morgan's Louisiana & Texas Railroad & Steamship Company. In 1887, he became general manager of Southern Pacific's Texas and Louisiana Lines. Kruttschnitt was appointed by E.H. Harriman as vice president and general manager of the entire Southern Pacific Company. He oversaw not only Southern Pacific but Union Pacific railroad as well. All new railroad construction was approved by Kruttschnitt before being sent to Harriman for final approval. Kruttschnitt played a major role in establishing the railroad's common standards. Subsequently,

Water well used for irrigating rice, 1911. *Photo courtesy of Freeman Archives and the excellent staff at the Acadia Parish Library in Crowley, Louisiana.*

Steam pumps were prevalent in the late 1800s and early to mid-1900s. *Photo courtesy of Freeman Archives and the excellent staff at the Acadia Parish Library in Crowley, Louisiana.*

the number of items for inventory was reduced; standardized equipment was interchangeable, which reduced downtime; larger-volume orders resulted in lower costs; and standardized equipment could be quickly moved from one area to another as needed. Julius Kruttschnitt died only days after his retirement. He was so well respected that when he died on May 31, 1925, all Southern Pacific trains, ferries and ships paused in his honor.

Union Pacific and Southern Pacific were unmerged or separated into individual railroad entities (for the first time) on April 1, 1913. I digressed a bit to tell you about one of the greatest railroaders from Louisiana; now, back to the construction of the Midland Branch.

January 4, 1896

"The roads west of here leading to the Gueydan settlement are in a horrible condition. Seller's lane is an impossible bog hole, and the road overseer evidently is waiting for the grand jury to indict him before he fixes it." —*Abbeville Meridional*

February 1, 1896

"Southern Pacific Railroad linemen began work last week putting up the telegraph line between Crowley and Gueydan." —*Jennings Times*. Lumber for the depot at Gueydan had been on the ground for some time, and it was expected that work on its construction would commence soon. It seems that the railroad company and townspeople weren't gee-hawing on the location. The depot was said to be forty feet by one hundred feet.

September 26, 1896

The headlines in the *Crowley Signal* read: "J.P. Gueydan left for New Orleans on Monday, where he will remain some time under medical treatment." Gueydan had not been feeling his best for the past couple of weeks, the newspaper reported. His son, Eugene Gueydan, accompanied his father to the city. —*Crowley Signal*

November 14, 1896

The *Crowley Signal* reported that a Methodist church would soon be built in Gueydan. The newspaper also reported that "Rev. G.W.L. Smith, accompanied by Rev. Woodson, of Jennings, went down there several days ago and selected lots for the building, which will front on the town park side."

Steam pump bringing water to irrigate rice. *Photo courtesy of Freeman Archives and Acadia Parish Library in Crowley, Louisiana.*

December 19, 1896

The *Meridional* reported that "the Gueydan rice lands, along the canal with water assured, are now for rent for 1897." The article advised that anyone interested should apply to "B.M. Lambert or A. Kaplan, Crowley, La." An article in the *Meridional* of Saturday, July 28, 1900, advised farmers and shippers of a new rice rate issued by Southern Pacific Railroad between Louisiana points and New Orleans. However, the new rate wasn't published. During that era, the Railroad Commission of Louisiana established railroad freight rates. It was the precursor of the Public Service Commission, which historically was a stepping stone toward becoming a candidate for governor.

November 20, 1900

The *Gueydan Journal* reported on Pierre Gueydan's death, stating that before his death, he became an American citizen. Mr. Gueydan "died in Marseilles, France, while waiting to embark on a ship returning to America."

April 27, 1901

The *Meridional* reported that lot sales in Gueydan the previous Monday and Tuesday did fine, and it was well attended. "The total sales amounted to more than $10,000."

June 15, 1901

The *Gueydan News* reported that "during the last ten months, Southern Pacific Railroad earned $64,197,860.00." The above was also reported by the *Abbeville Meridional* newspaper.

June 15, 1901

"First dirt was broken at Gueydan last Monday on the extension of the railroad from Gueydan to Abbeville." —*Abbeville Meridional*

February 1, 1902

The *Abbeville Herald* reported on the status of the railroad between Abbeville and Gueydan. It stated that the bridge over the Vermilion River west of the depot had been completed Sunday and tested Monday. However, there was still a few more days' work to be done before allowing trains to run west of Abbeville. By May 10, 1902, a new railroad schedule for the Midland Branch was posted. "Westbound Passenger train #70 leave New Iberia 1:15 p.m. and arrive Eunice 5:50 p.m. Eastbound Passenger train #71 leave Eunice 7:15 a.m. and arrive New Iberia 11:50 a.m." There was also a timetable for freight train no. 73 westbound and no. 72 eastbound.

Historically, on the Southern Pacific Railroad, eastward trains were invariably identified by even numbers, and westward trains were always identified by odd numbers. This applied to main track trains as well as branch line trains, no matter what actual or physical direction the tracks went toward. This was also true for mile markers on the SPRR: for instance, Algiers was mile post 0, and the mile post numbers increased in number as you moved westward or away from Algiers.

June 14, 1902

Tucked away in an article, it was mentioned that Southern Pacific Railroad had completed the last segment of the branch line between Abbeville and Gueydan on May 1, 1902. This completed the entire Midland Branch. To give readers a flavor of what would happen once the Midland Branch was completely built from end to end, the *Meridional* reported: "A. Saporito purchased four lots on State Street 'two squares' below the railroad in [F.A.

Shocking rice in Cajun Country. *Photo courtesy of Freeman Archives and the wonderful staff at the Acadia Parish Library in Crowley, Louisiana.*

Godchaux addition] on the right-hand side": Saporito paid $950 for all four lots. It was probably considered a good price. Also, in the same newspaper: "There is talk of fencing in Magdalene Square and planting trees and flowers and making walks through it thus converting it into a park. What a beautiful place it would make."

Another interesting newspaper article in the *Meridional* of August 9, 1902, reported that by this time, the economic depression that began in 1893 was over. Things were looking bright; area businesses were flourishing and store shelves were full of items people could not readily get before the railroads. Some of the first pioneers to arrive in the Gueydan area, as mentioned earlier, were the settlers from Union and Parke County Indiana: e.g., the Gillentine family. They arrived sometime in 1894, compliments of ads from Southern Pacific Railroad and the Duson brothers. And as reported by the *Gueydan Journal*, John Thomas and his wife, the former Mary Susan Maines, established the first store in Wright. John also managed the Garland estate at Wright. A post office was also established there. In 1897, John built the first rice warehouse in Gueydan. Another early arrival was the William Lafayette Doss family. The Dosses arrived in 1897 and established the first general merchandise business in the sixth structure erected in Gueydan. William

Unloading rice in Gueydan, 1897. *Photo courtesy of Helen Gaspard Hayes, local historian and preservationist. Without historians such as Ms. Helen, we would only have the here and the right now—no history.*

Doss was soon elected to the Vermilion Parish school board. He managed the local school as well as selecting its teachers. Doss was also involved in other community activities. A year later (1898), brothers Abel and Edgar Toups along with their uncle Firman settled in Gueydan and became businessmen. Able had a confectionery, while Edward was a pharmacist. In 1903, another area business opened: the Gueydan Machine Shop. The proprietors were G.W. Booze and Mr. Wainwright. The Curtis family was also an early arrival to Gueydan. T.J. Curtis was a former mayor of Gueydan from 1903 to 1907. The Rizzuto family, originally from Sicily, migrated to American at the beginning of the twentieth century and settled in Gueydan in the early 1900s. I would be remiss if I didn't mention Espera "Oscar" DiCorti, the son of Italian-born immigrants—Iron Eyes Cody. Iron Eyes became a genuine Hollywood-created "Cherokee Indian" who starred in numerous western movies over the years. You might remember him best in a 1980s Keep America Beautiful public service announcement, where he shed tears after seeing all the litter in our waterways.

MANY THANKS GO TO the various newspapers and archives—the *Gueydan Journal*, the *Crowley Signal*, the *Jennings Daily Journal* and especially the Newspaper Archive—for their continuous collection and preservation of our history. Thanks also goes to the many people who have generously shared photo images for this work. I appreciate it and will forever be grateful to you. *Merci Cher!*

Chapter 10

MEMORIES OF OLE HANK

I t all started with a knock on the door one Sunday morning about seventy-five years ago while she was living in New Orleans, said Millie (Guillot) Powell, a ninety-five-year-old native of Marksville, Louisiana. When Millie opened the door to see who it was, there stood a gangly and disheveled man wearing a filthy white shirt partially opened and a badly stained Stetson. "Good morning, ma'am. I'm here to see Danny Powell," said the gaunt stranger. Millie said the cowboy looked like a bum. "If he's Hank Williams, I'm Betty Grable," she said to her husband, Danny Powell, who immediately sprang upright and bolted to the front door. Hank entered the Bank Street duplex just off Carrollton Avenue and sat on the couch with his long, skinny legs crossed.

Millie vividly remembered seeing a large hole in the sole of his boot. "It was about the size of a quarter," said Millie. "And his breath reeked of liquor and cigarette smoke." Millie's husband, Danny, was a talented self-taught musician originally from Florida. "He could play nearly any instrument," said Millie. He was an especially gifted fiddle player, having won numerous accolades. Danny was highly sought after and had played with many well-known country bands in Nashville and other parts of the country. At the time, Danny was the leader of the Country Boys, a country band. And at one time, he had several bands. Danny played fiddle, while Millie played drums. Back then, they played country music all around the New Orleans area. Millie remembered playing music on Sunday afternoons at the Harmony Inn and the Silver Star in New Orleans, among many other venues. They also played across the Mississippi River on the west bank at the Moulin Rouge and the Gay Paree on Fourth Street in Marrero and the Keyhole, which was also on Fourth Street but in Westwego, which at that time was owned by L.J. Sarton of Brookhaven, Mississippi. In addition to the above dance halls, they also performed live on radio shows at WWL, the big 870 and at WTPS (1240 AM) which was on Lee Circle. It was later converted to a museum.

Hank Williams had known Danny Powell since their days in Nashville. "Back then Danny brought the house down with his rendition of 'The Mockingbird,'" said Millie. She said that Danny sounded a lot like Eddie Arnold. I tried to find the origin of the song but could not. If it is the correct "Mockingbird Song," it was rerecorded in the summer of 1963 by two groups: Inez and Charley Foxx, a brother-sister duo. Their song was recorded in 1963 and was quite successful on the music charts. Aretha Franklin also recorded it in 1963 on her album *Running Out of Fools*. Sometime in the 1970s, the "Mockingbird Song" was recorded by Carly Simon and James Taylor, and the latest to record the "Mockingbird Song" was Toby Keith and his daughter Krystal on Keith's *Greatest Hits Volume 2* album in 2004. I digressed a bit to tell you about the "Mockingbird Song." Now back to Ole Hank.

At the time of Hank's visit in New Orleans, he was trying to hire local musicians for his band, and Danny Powell was his connection. After visiting with Danny and Millie that Sunday morning, which was probably sometime in the late 1940s or early 1950s, Hank suggested they go looking for musicians. During that era, many of the local musicians of New Orleans hung out on St. Charles Street after playing their nightly gigs. Millie got into the back seat of "Hank's Cadillac limousine," where she noticed papers stuffed inside a pouch behind the front seat. To her amazement, scrawled on a sheet of paper were the lyrics of "Last Night, I Heard You Crying in Your Sleep," which was recorded in 1947. Later that evening, they ended up playing music on the west bank at the Gay Paree. Millie played drums during their performance, with Danny on vocals and fiddle. On the electric steel was someone they called Pee-Wee. On rhythm guitar and vocals was Roger Augustine, who Millie said sounded remarkably like Ernest Tubb. Woody Mackey played electric bass guitar while ole Hank sang a few of his hit songs. At the time, Danny's band was nonunion, while Hank belonged to a union, so for that reason, he didn't play for long, just long enough to fire up the enthusiastic crowd for Danny and Millie's country band.

Sometime later, probably in 1951, Millie and Danny saw Hank again when he was at old Tulane Stadium with "Coozan Dud" (Dudley LeBlanc) and his Hadacol entourage. She still has the handkerchief autographed by

Millie and Danny Powell. *Photo courtesy of Cindy Powell.*

Hank Williams, Cesar Romero and many other celebrities that followed Coozan Dud. Hank Williams died on January 1, 1953, just as he was at the top of his profession. A short time later, Danny gave up playing music. He and Millie and their young daughter left New Orleans and moved to Indiana, where Danny returned to his day job. Danny worked a construction job on toll roads in Illinois, Ohio and Indiana, where Millie's second daughter was born.

Danny Powell died in 1974. Millie continued to live in New Orleans until after the devastation of Katrina (2005), a category 5 hurricane. She enjoys spending time with her grandchildren and great-grandchildren. Millie says anyone with rhythm can learn to play drums. She learned by beating the bottoms of cooking pots. Seriously!

Chapter 11

THE CURIOUS EXECUTIONS
OF WILLIE FRANCIS

L ike a true crime saga, the story of Willie Francis has all the elements of a thrilling novel—a whiff of intrigue, murder and suspense, along with a U.S. Supreme Court associate justice left forever troubled by his decision. Our story begins after the body of Andrew I. Thomas was found in his garage behind his home. The *Biloxi Daily Herald* of November 11, 1944, reported that Thomas was a fifty-four-year-old druggist who owned Thomas Drug Store in St. Martinville. He lived alone in the Evangeline Park Addition of town and was the victim of an apparent robbery gone terribly awry. He suffered one gunshot to the head and four more to the body—a bit overkill. There were signs of a struggle. His body was found sometime on Wednesday, November 8, 1944, but authorities believed he was murdered Tuesday night, the night before his body was found.

Over the years, I've read numerous times that when a victim is shot or stabbed multiple times or more than necessary to cause death—e.g., the way Andrew Thomas was murdered—this means that the victim knew his assailant quite well. Regardless, through newspaper articles, I learned that Thomas was a druggist in New Orleans for about ten years before moving to St. Martinville, where he was an established druggist for several years before his murder. He was the brother of St. Martinville police chief Claude Thomas, who was certainly involved with the murder investigation along with Sheriff E. Leonard Resweber and the Louisiana State Police. Andrew Thomas was buried in St. Michael Cemetery in St. Martinville. A number of people were questioned regarding the murder of Andrew Thomas, but none were charged with the gruesome murder. Police searched for any and all possible leads, to no avail. Days turned into weeks and weeks turned into months with no apprehension of the killer. An exhaustive nine months had gone by, and the case had gone cold.

Finally, on August 3, 1945, a month before the end of World War II, police in St. Martinville got a huge break that broke the case wide open. They received a phone call from police in Port Arthur, Texas, stating they had in their custody a person of interest they might want to question. It seems that a young man named Willie Francis had left St. Martinville to visit his sister in Port Arthur, Texas. A headline in the *Port Arthur News* of August 6, 1945, reported the arrest of Willie Francis from St. Martinville. On August 2, 1944, while authorities in Texas were searching for illegal drug smugglers, Willie Francis happened by carrying a large suitcase they thought contained illegal drugs. Francis was taken to police headquarters for questioning, and as it turned out, no drugs were found. However, during their search, they found Andrew Thomas's identification in Willie Francis's wallet. As Port Arthur city detective E. Oster continued questioning Francis, he began to stutter, which, to the detectives, meant he was lying or trying to cover up something. One thing led to another, and before long, Francis confessed to the St. Martinville robbery and subsequent murder, which netted him a sum total of four dollars and a watch.

There was no scientific evidence used against Francis at that time that could link him to the murder. It was long before DNA testing. The only evidence against Francis was Thomas's driver's license and wristwatch and his confession of having killed Thomas. Francis signed a sworn statement stating that it was he who had, in fact, killed Andrew Thomas approximately nine months earlier. He also admitted to stealing a .38 handgun for the planned robbery. Francis was extradited to St. Martinville and charged with the horrific murder of Andrew Thomas. He was locked behind an iron door and steel bars. His attorney at the time was James Skelly Wright. Francis was housed in the New Iberia jail for safekeeping. Sixteen-year-old Willie Francis's trial was held Thursday, September 13, 1945, the same month that the Japanese surrendered. The *Port Arthur News* of September 16, 1945, reported that the two law enforcement officers who apprehended and questioned Francis in Port Arthur in August 1944 testified at Willie Francis's murder trial. They were Port Arthur city detective E. Oster and justice of the peace E.L. Canada. Francis was found guilty and convicted by an all-White jury after only fifteen minutes of deliberations. Francis was convicted of murder and was sentenced to die in the state's electric chair.

Willie Francis was reported to be barely literate, the youngest of thirteen children from the community of St. Martinville. The day of his scheduled electrocution was Friday, May 3, 1946. Back during that era, each parish held its own electrocutions, but the state provided the mobile electric chair—dubbed Gruesome Gertie—and the state supervised its operation. After Willie Francis was strapped to the chair, Sheriff Resweber of St. Martin Parish asked him if he had anything to say about anything. Willie was probably frightened out of his mind, too scared to say anything. The hood or death mask was placed over his head. The officials in charge of the electrocution flipped a switch to energize the electrical apparatus attached to Willie Francis.

At that very moment, Willie Francis's lips puffed out, his body squirmed and tensed and he jumped as the chair rocked on the floor. The *Daily Advertiser* of May 4, 1946, reported that the condemned man said: "Take it off, take it off." The switch was then turned off. Some of the men left, and a few minutes later, Sheriff Resweber came in and announced that the governor had granted Francis a reprieve due to the electrocution malfunction. Instead of being zapped with thousands of volts of electricity, he felt only a slight tingling sensation. The *Daily Advertiser* of Lafayette reported that after Willie Francis's botched electrocution, he said, "Thomas was a swell guy" and "I don't know why I shot him because I wasn't after money." Later, Francis showed news reporters an inscription he made a month earlier on the cell wall, which read: Practically I killed Andrew by accident. It will happen once in a lifetime. Look where Andrew is today, he's in a lonely cold grave. Of course, I'm not a killer. Andrew Thomas is dead. Murder by Willie. Murder at midnight. Willie Francis 800 Washington Street, St. Martinville. Sorry at myself.

Willie Francis, the only man to ever walk away from an electric chair and live to talk about it, felt relieved—although temporarily. Francis was ambivalent; he had mixed feelings toward what had just happened and what might happen again in the not-too-distant future. Yes, he had walked away from the electric chair alive—but not free. The *Daily Advertiser* quoted Fred S. LeBlanc, the Louisiana attorney general, as saying, "There is one line of authority, which states that if a death sentence was not carried out on the date set, it could not be attempted again." LeBlanc pointed out that the "court's sentence probably said Francis should be executed until dead." And following that statement is a statement by D.D. Bazer, the prison warden at Angola, who said the electric chair that Willie Francis was strapped to malfunctioned when the switch was thrown. He said the electric chair had failed due to loose electrical connections in the control panel. The decision was made to take the chair to Baton Rouge for repairs, to be returned the following Thursday for another attempt at executing Willie Francis. If successful, the following day, the portable electric chair was scheduled to be delivered to Leesville for the execution of eighteen-year-old George Edward Jr. of Leesville, Louisiana, a Black man who was convicted of murdering Henry Roberts, a farmer near Leesville. In the same publication, it reported that Louisiana governor Jimmie Davis granted Francis a six-day reprieve.

However, five days later, the *Daily Advertiser* of May 9, 1946, reported that Louisiana Supreme Court chief justice Charles Austin O'Niell, Louisiana's twelfth state supreme court justice, granted a reprieve to Francis not to exceed thirty days. The court needed to study the case. By then, Bertrand DeBlanc (1911–1992), a young Lafayette attorney, thought the possibility of a second execution was cruel and unusual and took Willie Francis's case. DeBlanc thought subjecting Francis to yet another electrocution attempt was just wrong. I had always heard that if a person is sentenced to be electrocuted and something happens through no fault of the condemned, he was supposed to be released due to it was an act of God. Wasn't it James Madison, our fourth president and one of the Founding Fathers of the United States, who said, "No person shall be subject to more than one punishment or one trial for the same offense"? According to the excellent book *A People's History of the Supreme Court* by Peter Irons, Willie Francis should have been protected by the double jeopardy clause of the Fifth Amendment and the cruel and unusual punishment clause of the Eighth Amendment.

Meanwhile, over in Vernon Parish, Sheriff W.C. Turner was preparing for an execution of his own. The *Monroe News-Star* of May 10, 1946, reported that Sheriff Turner was preparing for the electrocution of George Edward Jr., who was convicted of ambushing, shooting and robbing a farmer with a .22 rifle in December 1945, which netted him about five dollars. Edward's execution was scheduled for May 10 between the hours of one and three o'clock in the afternoon, as required by the death warrant. Sheriff Turner was preparing for the execution to go off without a hitch. According to the *Monroe News-Star*, Edwards had received a last-minute reprieve on February 23, "when the Louisiana Supreme court asked for additional time to study an appeal in his case." In the meantime, Sheriff Turner had the electric chair in his jail since it was repaired in Baton Rouge. The chair had been tested and was sitting on go. I digressed a bit to tell you about George Edward Jr. and his arrangement with destiny.

The *Daily Advertiser* of May 15, 1946, reported that by a unanimous decree, Louisiana's high court denied Bertrand DeBlanc's request to halt his client's plea. The Louisiana Supreme Court held that Francis was legally in the custody of Sheriff Leonard Resweber of St. Martin Parish. It also stated that the "court had no authority to set aside the order of execution, nor to order a pardon or commutation of sentence." The court also refused to act further on a decision by District Judge James D. Simon of St. Martinville, who denied Francis's writs.

An article in the Associated Press of January 14, 1947, from Washington, D.C., which was also published in the *Daily Advertiser*, reported an anonymous letter simply addressed to "Willie Francis, Jailhouse, New Iberia," which was quite long. The letter began with, "Dear Willie, I thought you'd like to know how it was when nine men you never saw sitting in a marble palace talked about your future." The letter writer went on and informed Francis about the U.S. Supreme Court building and how grand it was. "It's all marble, not like any court you ever saw down there in bayou country." The letter stated, "Before you were making history, your case is what lawyers call historic. Nothing like it had happened before." The letter writer also spoke about the 5–4 decision and spoke of Associate Justice Felix Frankfurter. According to the anonymous author of the letter, Frankfurter said that Francis's earlier attempted execution was an "innocent misadventure." The author said he thought Francis would like to know that bit of information. He also thought Francis would like to know that Frankfurter allegedly said, "The whole situation was very disturbing." Frankfurter was one of five U.S. Supreme Court justices against Francis who said a second attempt at electrocution was not cruel and unusual punishment. Justice Frankfurter retired in August 1962. Indeed, Felix Frankfurter did say, years later, that he was deeply affected by his decision.

The *Daily Advertiser* of January 14, 1947, reported that Francis said, "Death and me is old neighbors. But remember this, I'm a closer neighbor of the Lord." Attorney Bertrand DeBlanc said in an interview that his client was much calmer now than he was after walking away for the electric chair. He also stated that even though the U.S. Supreme Court ruled 5–4 against Francis, he still had a chance. The Lafayette attorney wasn't giving up; he said he would file another motion for yet another new hearing. An Associated Press article of Tuesday, January 14, 1947, datelined New Iberia, reported that Willie Francis was calm when he learned of the 5–4 ruling against him by the U.S. Supreme Court. The ruling came down on the day after Francis's birthday. Francis was apparently making comments about his upcoming second attempt in the electric chair when he said, "I always sort of wondered if I was a brave man. Now I guess maybe I'm going to find out. I'm 'gonna' find out the hard way, boss, so there won't be no doubt in my mind when I leave." He continued by indicating that a lot of men never find out if they are brave. Some wonder if they are the man they thought they were. After his attorney informed Francis of another motion filed, Francis said, "It's the same thing. The same old thing. A man's got to die sometime, and I reckon my time has plumb done come." Francis made the same statement earlier when Iberia Parish sheriff Gilbert Ozenne informed him of the 5–4 decision. Francis refused when the sheriff asked if he wanted him to let his family members know of the court decision.

Louisiana governor Jimmie H. Davis said he would sign another death warrant as soon as he received the high court's judicial mandamus giving the state the green signal to proceed with the second attempt at electrocuting Francis. In the eyes of the high court, a second trip to the electric chair was not "cruel and unusual punishment." The *Daily Advertiser* of January 16, 1947, stated that Bertrand DeBlanc, by now a national figure, showed Francis the telegram from Washington and told him about a totally disabled war veteran who offered to sit in the chair for him. Meanwhile, Francis, in his own right, was enjoying something akin to celebrity status throughout most of the country. He was surprised that someone would offer to do that for him. According to the publication, the disabled veteran was former Army Corps of Engineers captain John F. Kenny of Washington, D.C. The wife of the war veteran said, "My husband, former Captain, Army Corps of Engineers, now very probably permanently and totally disabled from service [during] World War II and unable to obtain any consideration from the Veterans Administration, now volunteers to go to an electric chair for Willie Francis." Of course, the disabled veteran knew it was impossible, but he felt it would comfort Willie Francis knowing that a complete stranger was willing to sit in the chair for him. When Francis was informed of this by DeBlanc, Willie responded by saying, "Oh, no! Tell him thanks, if anybody's 'gonna' sit, I'll sit."

The Associated Press also reported receiving telegrams from Mississippi pleading for clemency for Willie Francis. It prompted Jefferson Davis, executive assistant to the governor of Mississippi, to respond to the telegrams, saying, "The office of the governor of Mississippi yesterday strived to make it clear that Willie Francis is not under jurisdiction of this state. 'We get enough telegrams on Mississippi cases,'" said Davis. He continued by stating,

"We wish persons in other states would realize that Willie is not a Mississippi case. We have enough troubles of our own."

The *Daily Advertiser* of May 8, 1947, reported that "Lafayette attorney Bertrand DeBlanc assisted by James S. Wright, a Washington attorney, tried to sway the high court with two new moves to stay Willie Francis's execution." New evidence was submitted to the high court, purportedly showing that during Francis's first execution attempt, the executioner and others were drunk, "so drunk that it was impossible for them to have known what they were doing." The source of this information was an affidavit belonging to former judge Louis M. Cyr of New Iberia. The petition stated: "The scene was a disgraceful and inhuman exhibition, that as soon as the switch controlling the current was taken off, the drunkard executioner cursed Francis and told him he would be back to finish electrocuting him, and if the electricity did not kill him, he would kill him with a rock."

Attorney Wright asked the Supreme Court "to issue a writ of habeas corpus on behalf of Francis and suggested that the high tribunal order that the facts surrounding the first execution attempt be determined by a commission appointed by the court or by a district judge in Louisiana." Wright's petition stated that Francis alleged the executioner "was actuated by sadistic impulses and either willfully, deliberately, or intentionally applied less than minimal lethal current." Meanwhile, DeBlanc filed a second petition that day (May 8, 1947) asking the tribunal to review the refusal of the Louisiana Supreme Court's decision to grant Francis a writ of habeas corpus. Try as the two attorneys might, the U.S. Supreme Court rejected their last-minute attempts to save Francis. The high tribunal said "its actions were without prejudice," meaning the case could come up again on a later date. Thus, attorneys for Francis could carry their "grave new" allegations to Louisiana courts. Asking DeBlanc to carry his newly discovered evidence back to Louisiana indicated that at least one of the Supreme Court justices regretted his earlier 5–4 decision against Willie Francis. In all likelihood, that one justice may have been Felix Frankfurter.

The *Daily Advertiser* of May 9, 1947, reported that Willie Francis was transported from New Iberia to St. Martinville at eight o'clock in the morning on May 9, 1947, as a small crowd began to assemble outside the jail yard. The newspaper reported that seven members of Francis's family had visited him the day before while in New Iberia. After the visit, his mother left for Beaumont, Texas, to visit her daughter. On the morning of May 9, Bertrand DeBlanc visited his client in his tiny cell in St. Martinville at 10:15, just two hours before Francis's scheduled execution. The Lafayette attorney, "haggard and sleepy-eyed," felt that he could possibly secure another stay, but his client told him to let it go. He had enough; it was time. Willie Francis "practiced walking the short last mile so that he could 'die like a man.'" A crowd of perhaps five hundred gathered outside under the shade of a huge oak tree, which was next to the red brick, two-story jail that housed Francis. Among the witnesses was Claude Thomas, the brother of Andrew, who was killed by Francis on the night of November 7, 1944. Back then, Claude Thomas was the police chief of St. Martinville. Claude was the only member of the family that was present for the execution.

Francis smiled as he sat in the same electric chair as a year earlier. The time was 12:02 p.m. Central Standard Time when he was strapped in. The switch was thrown at 12:05 p.m., and at 12:10 p.m., Willie Francis was pronounced dead. Bertrand DeBlanc had gone twice to the U.S. Supreme Court, three times to the Louisiana Supreme Court and three times to the state pardon board, all in an attempt to save the life of Willie Francis. If DeBlanc had taken his "grave new" evidence to Louisiana's high court, would it have changed anything? Probably not.

It's been said that Associate Justice Felix Frankfurter regretted voting against his conscience and in favor of sending Willie Francis to the electric chair a second time. His was the fifth and deciding vote against Francis, a decision that haunted Frankfurter probably for the rest of his life.

When Willie Francis died after his historic second electrocution, so did the belief that a condemned man's life would be spared if an accident occurred that stopped the execution. We now know it's a false assumption or at least an urban myth to believe a person's life would be saved. In 1947, Willie Francis made the top ten news stories for the state of Louisiana—it was actually number five. The September Hurricane was the top story. This was before named storms, and it was the first hurricane to strike New Orleans since 1915.

Chapter 12

THE DAY THE TRAINS STOPPED

On September 29, 1897, a group of medical doctors from New Orleans, including Dr. S.R. Oliphant, president of the Louisiana state board of health, and Dr. Guiteras, "the celebrated yellow fever expert," boarded a train to attend a yellow fever conference the following day in Beaumont, Texas. Tagging along was a who's who of noted celebrity-like hangers-on. The plan for the medical doctors was to meet other health officials from Louisiana and Texas to exchange ideas about the yellow fever epidemic. Their special train left New Orleans on time on the Southern Pacific Railroad and picked up other medical doctors along the way. Dr. Alfred Duperier of New Iberia was on board. He was one of the few survivors of the great unnamed hurricane that demolished Isle Dernière more than four decades earlier, in August 1856. The good doctor was a local hero after he saved lives following the destruction of the small island south of Houma, Louisiana. One of the survivors of the killer storm later became Mrs. Duperier.

The doctors' special also picked up ex-sheriff Frere of St. Mary Parish, and also on board were Southern Pacific Railroad division superintendent Owens of Algiers and a number of others.

By afternoon, the doctors' special had gone by Lafayette, and all was proceeding well. That was until the train arrived at the east city limits of Rayne. The train came to an abrupt halt after a group of armed townspeople flagged the train to stop. The town folks of Rayne informed Locomotive Engineer Gregory of their yellow fever quarantine. They would not allow any trains to go through the town for fear of contaminating its citizens.

The following morning, the headline in the *Houston Daily Post* read, "The Way Was Barred." Officials on the train tried to speak to the "armed mob" of shotgun-wielding men, to no avail. Passengers on the train were infuriated when they were informed "under no circumstances would it be permitted to enter the corporate limits of Rayne." The mob was only concerned with the townspeople remaining safe from yellow fever. The group of citizens holding shotguns and rifles pointed their weapons at the locomotive engineer, informing him this was as far as his train was going. The armed men "threatened to tear up the track if the train persisted to run through town." An "unsuspecting fellow walked from the depot at Rayne and entered the train to deliver a telegram to one of the physicians." The unfortunate man was forced to stay with the train. Rayne's quarantine instructions were simple: no one goes in, and no one comes out.

The special train made it back to Lafayette by six o'clock and stayed just long enough to take on water and coal for the engine. According to *Lafayette Gazette* of October 2, 1897, the train returned to New Orleans after the doctors on board the train were informed that other towns had implemented quarantines, including Opelousas, Crowley and Lake Charles. The doctor's special arrived in New Orleans in the wee hours of the next morning. There was "a deal of unfavorable comment" pertaining to the armed citizens of Rayne. This put an end to the yellow fever conference.

Newton's law of physics says: for every action, there is an equal and opposite reaction. No one knows with any certainty what adverse effects were caused when the train was turned back. Family members of Herman Venable (1940–2022), originally from Church Point, weren't told why they couldn't board the train. They found out many years later why. As the story goes, Herman Venable's great-uncle Delmar Rivet from Branch in northern Acadia Parish was ten years old at the time. He had an appointment to see a medical specialist in New Orleans about his cleft palate. The family were never told why they couldn't board the train that fateful day in 1897. Herman said his uncle had one of the most severe cases of cleft palate he had ever seen. Because of the yellow fever quarantine in Rayne, they could not make the scheduled appointment, and Rivet never had the operation. He lived a very productive life. He spoke no English, and his wife spoke no French. Regardless of the language barrier, they had two children. I digressed a bit to tell you about Delmar Rivet; now, back to the yellow fever.

In a series of nineteenth-century yellow fever outbreaks, there were over forty-one thousand deaths in New Orleans alone. In September 1897, the city of New Orleans reported over four hundred deaths caused by the yellow fever epidemic; however, none were reported the previous eight years, which caused grave concern to a lot of people, including the folks of Rayne. That was the reason for the quarantine.

Two days after the incident in Rayne, the front page of the *Daily Picayune* was plastered with a long-winded article written about the unceremonious reception and mistreatment received by the good doctors of New Orleans and how they were threatened with violence and forced at gunpoint to turn around. The health officials used harsh words when referring to the townspeople of Rayne, saying they were nothing more than "a mob of armed citizens" who were "ill-advised and uninformed." Not to be outdone, New Orleans city officials expressed their disgust with the town in Acadia Parish, saying the townspeople displayed ignorance and "home rule with a vengeance." Of course, this was all said while under the cover of safety and many miles from Rayne. *Home rule* is a term that dates to the colonial period in America. Many states had home rule, which gave local municipalities the power to exercise self-government in a limited way.

Other towns along the railroad lines followed suit and imposed their own brand of quarantine. And as a result, the Southern Pacific and Texas Pacific Railroads, among others, laid off many of their workers because the only trains rolling were the noninfectious freights. The famous Sunset Limited suspended passenger rail service to New Orleans indefinitely due to the outbreak. Many city officials demanded an end to the recently imposed quarantines brought on by every hamlet, town, county or parish in the state. They wanted a reasonable and uniform national system of quarantine. In the affected areas, many blamed the quarantines for the deaths of some that were barred from seeking much-needed medical attention. Lawyers were consulted; officials were petitioned for a writ of habeas corpus to secure their release on the constitutional grounds that no man should be deprived of his liberty without a fair trial. The infected wanted to leave and seek medical treatment, while everyone else wanted to stop the people and stay in place to prevent the spread of yellow fever. It was a catch-22, or what some would refer to as a paradoxical situation.

There were numerous bogus allegations reported of yellow fever outbreaks. Calcasieu Parish passed an ordinance imposing a one-hundred-dollar fine on anyone convicted of malicious and willful circulation of false yellow fever rumors, and Louisiana governor Foster (the first one) issued a proclamation against panic, saying that fright killed more people than yellow fever. An old sea captain who once sailed between Havana, Cuba, and Charleston, South Carolina, gave his preventive remedy that he and

Several members of the Southern Pacific Railroad retiree luncheon at Dwight's Restaurant in Lafayette, Louisiana, circa pre-COVID. *Standing, left to right*: Milton Wyble, Carl Lastrapes, Don Bejeaux, the author, Marshall Cloteaux, John "J.W." Broussard, William "Bill" Lamar, Robert Bertrand, Pete Martin, Roy Martin, Jimmy Abboud, Stan Plunkett, Donald Vincent. *Seated, left to right*: Francis Castille, Merlin Robin, Roger Ohlsson, Johnny Gross and Terry Van Epps. We hope you've enjoyed the ride. *Author's collection.*

his crew used for thirty-three years to ward off yellow fever. He mixed a teaspoonful of pulverized charcoal with a tumbler full of water and drank it three or four times a week. Walter C. Flower, the mayor of New Orleans, predicted that the epidemic would be over in a matter of weeks. It lasted until 1905.

ABOUT THE AUTHOR

William Thibodeaux is a native of Rayne, Louisiana. While in high school, he did the unthinkable: he quit school to join the navy. He did quit school, but he never quit learning. In fact, he credits the military as the place where he began his love of books and learning. Some would call it nontraditional learning. He served onboard a World War II Fletcher-class destroyer—the USS *O'Bannon* (DD-450), which spent much of its time in the West Pacific. After his military obligations, William took a job with Southern Pacific Railroad beginning in 1970. He began his employment as a gandy dancer (track laborer), repairing the railroad, performing maintenance on the track structure and inspecting the railroad for defects. He held several supervisory positions, but mostly he was a roadmaster (engineering manager) with SPRR. Glory days! After the railroad merger, William held the same position but a different title with Union Pacific Railroad's Livonia Service Unit. He retired with more than forty-four years of combined loyal, dedicated and injury free-service.

In 2019, William was inducted into the Order of Living Legends for his dedication to the Acadian language and culture. Since 2010, he's been the facilitator for La Table Cadien de Rayne, a weekly gathering of people striving to preserve the Acadian language and culture. And since 2015, he has hosted Acadiana Memories, a monthly history program in Lafayette where participants reminisce about people, places and events of long ago. William is married to the former Judy Clark of Morse/Riceville, a graduate of Gueydan High School. She is the love of his life. They make their home in Lafayette, Louisiana. William is the author of *Hidden History of Acadiana*, *Historic Tales of Acadiana* and now *Cajun Country Chronicles*. They are his legacy.